Securing Startups

OrangeBooks Publication

1st Floor, Rajhans Arcade, Mall Road, Kohka, Bhilai, Chhattisgarh 490020

Website: **www.orangebooks.in**

First Edition, 2025

ISBN: 978-93-6554-898-3

Price: Rs. 560.00

Printed in India

SECURING STARTUPS

"FROM IDEA TO IPO: SECURITY PRACTICES FOR EVERY STAGE"

SANIL NADKARNI & ANKIT AGARWAL

OrangeBooks Publication
www.orangebooks.in

Foreword

By Diego Souza – CISO, ProG Holding Inc. | Former CISO, Cummins | C-Suite Executive & Board Member

In today's hyperconnected, data-driven world, startups are not only expected to innovate fast—they're also expected to stay secure. Unfortunately, security is often an afterthought, buried under product releases, investor meetings, and growth metrics. That's where this book by Sanil Nadkarni comes in—a much-needed game-changer in the cybersecurity space tailored specifically for startups.

Securing Startups does something rare: it strips away the fluff and breaks down cybersecurity into actionable steps that a startup founder, DevOps engineer, or early-stage CTO can understand and implement without needing a PhD in InfoSec. Sanil has taken the years of battle-tested experience he gained while securing some of the world's most complex environments—including his tenure as CISO at high-growth startups—and translated that into a guide that's both technically sound and strategically insightful.

What makes this book truly stand out is its clarity. Sanil doesn't just talk about protecting sensitive data or complying with frameworks—he walks you through how to actually do it, even with limited resources. Whether it's building your first security policy, implementing DevSecOps, or preparing for ISO/SOC compliance, this book equips you with frameworks and mindsets to take proactive control.

In an era where a single breach can sink an entire startup, Securing Startups should be on every founder's desk. It's more than just a manual—it's a survival toolkit. If you're serious about building a resilient, investor-ready, and customer-trusted startup, this book will be your playbook for secure innovation.

I've had the privilege of working with Sanil and witnessing his depth of knowledge and passion firsthand. He is a true security evangelist, and this book reflects his commitment to making cybersecurity practical, accessible, and impactful.

Read it. Apply it. And most importantly—secure your future.

Introduction

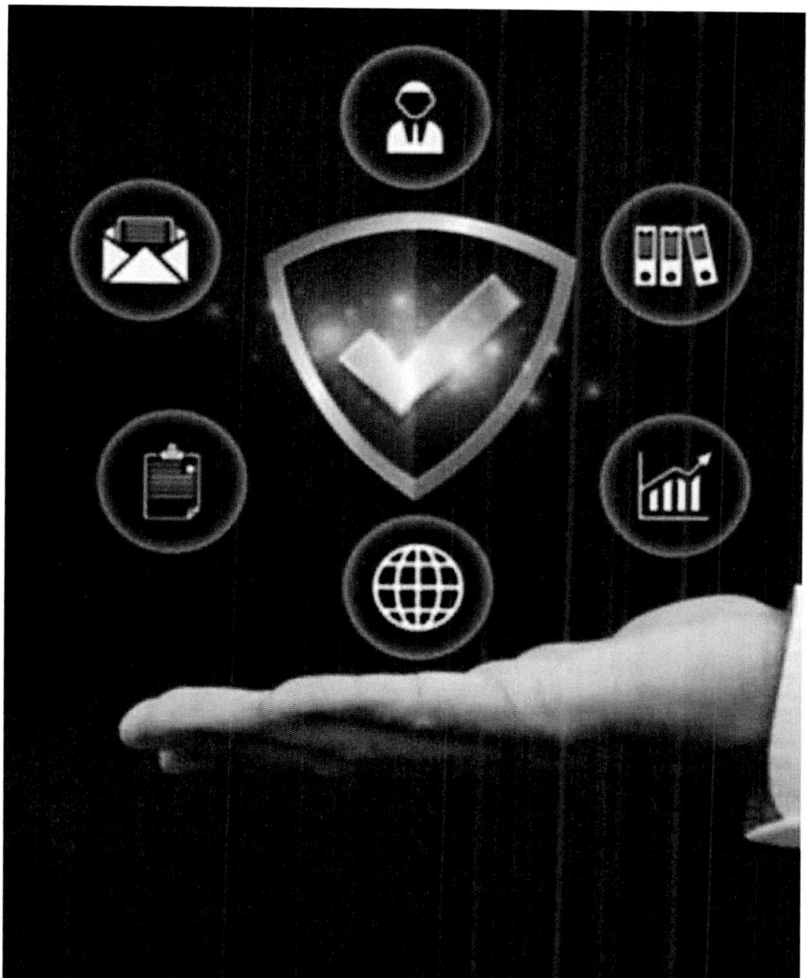

About The Author

I am Sanil Nadkarni, an executive powerhouse in cybersecurity with over 18 years of experience. My career has been devoted to fortifying the digital realm, where I have had the privilege of shaping and securing the landscape of tomorrow.

My educational journey began with completing my 12th grade at Mumbai University, followed by pursuing a bachelor's degree and a PhD in cybersecurity. I hold a leadership position at a multinational corporation, building on my experience as the Chief Information Security Officer (CISO) for Byju's, Heading Cyber Security for Cummins India, and several other esteemed companies.

I take immense pride in authoring the bestselling book, "Fundamentals of Information Security," a work that has been warmly embraced by students and colleagues alike. My passion for technology knows no bounds, and I proudly identify as a security evangelist.

In addition to my written contributions, I've had the privilege of sharing my insights through esteemed publications such as Computer Weekly, TechTarget, CIO India Review, CISO Platform, and U.S. Mortgage Banking. I am gradually extending my reach to seminars like the CISO Forum and Security Communities, where I serve as a faculty member.

My expertise lies in constructing robust information security frameworks and foundations for startups, IT/ITES, and banking institutions across diverse geographies. Along my journey, I've been honoured with several prestigious awards, further enriching my professional journey.

Outside of the cybersecurity realm, I am an avid reader who appreciates the profound impact of thought-provoking videos and enjoys the soothing melodies of the piano.

Thank you for taking the time to learn a bit about me, and I look forward to engaging in meaningful discussions and collaborations within the cybersecurity community and beyond.

Oh, yes—one quick view of the motivation behind my book:

You may be wondering what inspired me to undertake the writing of this book. Well, during my tenure as the CISO for the world's largest startup, I frequently found myself engaged in conversations with CTOs eager to enhance the security of their startups. However, it wasn't just CTOs who sought my expertise; DevOps engineers and developers also turned to me, struggling with the lack of accessible resources or literature on building cybersecurity from the ground up. This stark realisation ignited a powerful drive within me, compelling me to write this book. My mission is to inspire and guide CTOs, DevOps engineers, developers, and CISOs, equipping them to tackle the complex challenge of establishing cybersecurity measures for startups from the very foundation. This book aims to educate readers on the crucial importance of cybersecurity while also providing a roadmap for advancing a career in information security.

Designed for both working professionals and young students, this book is crafted to be easily understood in a single read. Written to reach a broad audience, it is straightforward, practical, and impactful.

Now that you're familiar with my objective, let's delve into why I wrote this book:

I consider myself incredibly fortunate because my "job," if you can even call it that, revolves around my genuine passion. I proudly embrace the title of security evangelist, a broad and encompassing term within the realm of information security. While I dedicate a significant portion of my time to speaking about cybersecurity at various conferences, sharing knowledge, and advocating for better security practices, there's a deep-seated desire within me to author a book aimed at guiding aspiring young professionals and students who aspire to excel in this field. The book is designed to confer on pivotal concepts, techniques, qualifications, certifications, employment opportunities, and thorough guidance and insight into cybersecurity.

Co-Author Of the Book

I am Ankit Agarwal as a seasoned IT leader with over 20 years of experience in IT security, governance, and risk management. I bring a wealth of expertise to the development of this book on securing startups. Currently, I serve as Vice President, Global Systems and Cyber Security @ Encora Inc. where I combine deep technical expertise with a strategic vision to elevate security practices across global operations.

I hold a Master of Technology (M.Tech) in Cloud Computing and Infrastructure, along with multiple industry-recognised certifications, including Project Management Professional (PMP), ITIL, and Microsoft Project and Portfolio Management. My extensive background includes consulting on various e-Governance projects for the Punjab State Government, where I spearheaded mission-critical initiatives to enhance the security of the State-wide Area Network. I collaborated with the Department of Information Technology (DoIT) and major multinational corporations to address business challenges, improve operational efficiency, and drive innovative security solutions.

Through this book, I aim to bridge the gap between complex security concepts and practical implementation, focusing on the unique needs and challenges that startups encounter. My mission is to offer clear, actionable guidance—whether you're a developer, DevOps engineer, or startup founder—enabling you to protect critical assets, achieve compliance, and foster secure, scalable growth.

This book is designed to be accessible and digestible, tailored for working professionals and aspiring students to read in one sitting. It covers key cybersecurity concepts, techniques, certifications, and career opportunities with a focus on startup environments. As a passionate security evangelist, I actively speak at conferences and engage with organisations that prioritise innovation and integrity. Through this work, I aspire to inspire the next generation of cybersecurity leaders and equip them with the tools needed to secure the future of their organisations.

With my co-authorship of this book, I hope to share valuable insights from my journey, helping startups build strong security foundations that foster trust, resilience, and long-term success in an ever-evolving digital world.

Acknowledgment

I've penned over 100 articles, yet my first book remains a labour of love and perseverance. This journey has been both challenging and extraordinary, and I owe it all to the incredible support I've received.

I begin with my deepest gratitude to my mother, to whom I dedicate this book. She was a remarkable woman who flawlessly balanced work and life. Her wisdom was profound; she often advised me to focus on the task at hand and not worry about the outcome. Her unwavering commitment to integrity, a principle she instilled in me, has been invaluable in the field of information security.

I also extend my heartfelt thanks to my father, my wife, and my brother. Their motivation and support have been my pillars of strength throughout this journey.

I would like to express my gratitude to my colleagues in the industry for taking the time to spread the book and also for taking the time to write a testimonial.

Throughout my journey in the corporate world, I encountered several inspirational leaders. Ten thousand chapters will not suffice if I list individuals who inspired me and had my back during this beautiful journey.

Sincere thanks to my team for being my constant support and contributing to making this a success. I am grateful to all my fantastic team members and the organisations I've worked with.

I owe a debt to my editor for ironing off the rough edges, which was instrumental in making this book look cool.

I am fortunate to have wonderful friends who keep feeding me the fib that my book will remain in good shape while simultaneously critiquing every tiny aspect of it.

Lastly, I would always like to be curious and learn more.

Index

Chapter - 1
Securing Startup Success

Secure your business: Cyber Security Strategies for Small Business Success

"At the end of the day, the goals are simple: safety and security."

- Jodi Rell

In the era of digitisation, where data holds a value akin to currency and cyber threats escalate daily, robust cybersecurity measures are imperative. This book emerges as a necessity—a guide shaped by years of experience in digital warfare, specifically tailored for Small and Medium-sized Enterprises (SMEs) and start-ups navigating the intricate landscape of cybersecurity.

As the Chief Information Security Officer (CISO) of a multinational corporation and an experienced author in cybersecurity, I've personally encountered the obstacles and risks that emerging business encounter when establishing a secure digital environment. This book serves as both a practical guide and a compass for those embarking on this often-daunting journey.

Building a cybersecurity team from scratch is no small feat. It requires a nuanced understanding of the cyber landscape, an acute awareness of the risks involved, and the foresight to anticipate and mitigate potential threats. This book aims to demystify the process, offering practical advice, real-world examples, and step-by-step guidance.

We will explore the foundational aspects of creating a cybersecurity team—identifying the key roles and skills required, understanding the importance of a diverse and dynamic team, and learning how to foster a culture of security awareness within your organization. Beyond team building, this book delves into the strategic implementation of cybersecurity controls, ensuring that your defences not only exist but are also practical and adaptable to the ever-evolving cyber threats.

This comprehensive guide transcends traditional book boundaries, offering a transformative exploration into the core of cybersecurity, specifically crafted to address the distinctive challenges and opportunities encountered by SMEs and startups. Whether you are a seasoned IT professional or a newcomer to the field, this invaluable resource equips you with the insights and tools essential for constructing a resilient and proactive cybersecurity framework. Embark on this journey with an open mind as we navigate the intricate yet rewarding realm of cybersecurity together. Your proactive steps today will shape the security and success of your business tomorrow.

Objectives

Upon completing this chapter, you will gain insight into:

- The Imperative of cybersecurity for startups.
- How to craft a strategic cybersecurity roadmap?

Overview: Securing Startup Success

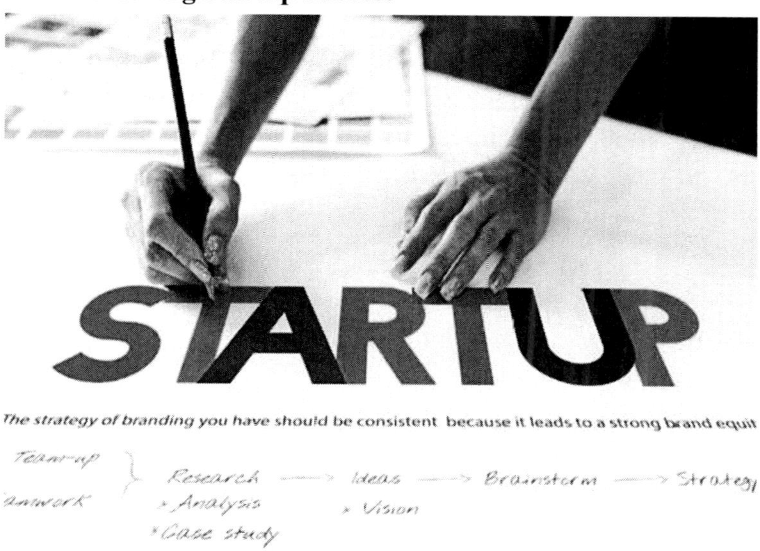

In this comprehensive guide, "Securing Startups," we undertake a crucial mission to empower small and medium-sized enterprises (SMEs) and startups with the knowledge and tools necessary to build and maintain a robust cybersecurity infrastructure. Meticulously crafted, this book addresses the unique challenges and resource constraints faced by smaller organisations. We begin by unravelling the complexities of cybersecurity, making it accessible and actionable for businesses without extensive technical backgrounds. The core of the book is dedicated to the practical aspects of forming a competent cybersecurity team, from identifying key roles and skill sets to integrating diverse perspectives for a well-rounded defence strategy.

We delve into the art of developing and implementing effective cybersecurity policies and controls, emphasising scalable and cost-effective solutions. Additionally, the book provides insights into navigating the regulatory landscape, managing cybersecurity risks, and fostering a culture of security awareness across all levels of the organisation. Through real-world case studies, expert interviews, and actionable checklists, this guide is an indispensable resource for SMEs and startups striving to fortify their digital fortresses in a landscape of ever-evolving cyber threats.

Whether you're at the helm of technological decisions, directly involved in cybersecurity implementation, or have a vested interest in the success of a tech startup, this book provides practical guidance and strategic insights to navigate the ever-evolving landscape of cybersecurity and secure your path to success.

At its core, cybersecurity is the practice of protecting systems, networks, and programs from digital attacks. These attacks often aim to access, change, or destroy sensitive information, extort money from users, or interrupt normal business processes. As we step into this realm, it's crucial to understand the basic terminology that forms the foundation of cybersecurity. Terms like 'malware,' which refers to malicious software designed to harm or exploit any programmable device or network, and 'phishing,' a method of tricking individuals into divulging sensitive information, are fundamental. Understanding these terms is not just about building a vocabulary; it's about laying the groundwork for a comprehensive understanding of the digital threats that businesses face.

Cyber Threat Spectrum

In today's interconnected world, the spectrum of cyber threats is vast and ever-evolving. Viruses, a type of malware that replicates by copying itself to other programs, and worms, which can spread without human interaction, are just the beginning. Ransomware, a critical term, involves malicious software that encrypts a victim's files and demands a ransom for restoration. The complexity of these threats highlights the necessity for robust cybersecurity measures. As we delve deeper, we encounter terms like 'cyber espionage,' which refers to using computer networks to gain illicit access to confidential information typically held by governments or other organisations. Understanding these diverse threats is the first step toward developing effective strategies to combat them.

Building a Cyber-Resilient Framework:

In the realm of cybersecurity, understanding strategies and mechanisms to safeguard against threats is crucial. Concepts like 'firewalls,' which monitor and control network traffic based on security rules, and 'encryption,' a method of converting data into code to prevent unauthorised access, play pivotal roles. Additionally, 'security protocols' encompass various standards and procedures designed to protect data integrity and confidentiality. In this digital age, where data breaches and cyber-attacks are increasingly common, grasping these concepts is critical for anyone looking to protect their digital assets effectively. As we explore these terms and concepts further, we lay the groundwork for building a resilient framework that can withstand the evolving landscape of cyber threats.

The Evolution of Cyber Threats: A Brief History and Current Landscape

In the Beginning, There Was the Floppy Disk

Once upon a time, in the ancient era of the 1980s, cyber threats were like mythical creatures - rare and almost unheard of. The first of their kind were more mischievous than menacing, often spread through the now archaic floppy disk. Picture this: you're rocking shoulder pads and big hair, blissfully unaware that the floppy disk you just shoved into your computer is about to display a cheeky message or, heaven forbid, play a little tune. These early viruses, while irritating, had all the malicious intent of a kitten playing with a ball of yarn. But oh, how times have changed!

The Internet Boom and Cyber Threats Go to College

Fast forward to the 90s, and the Internet is like the cool new kid on the block that everyone wants to hang out with. As we all flocked online, so did the cyber threats, getting smarter, sneakier, and more ambitious. This was the era of email viruses that promised love letters from secret admirers but delivered heartbreak in the form of crashed systems. Remember the 'I LOVE YOU' virus? It was like receiving a box of chocolates that exploded in your face. These threats made me understand the power of social engineering - because who can resist opening an email that says, "You've got to see this!"?

The Modern Menace - Smart, Sophisticated, and Slightly Terrifying

Here we are in the 21st century, and cyber threats have graduated with honours in deviousness. They've moved on from floppy disks to cloud storage, and their focus is no longer solely on humour. Today, we've got ransomware that holds your precious data hostage, demanding Bitcoin as if it's some sort of digital mafia boss. Then there are phishing scams so clever they could sell ice to Eskimos. And let's not forget the insidious world of spyware, lurking in the shadows, watching every move you make like a creepy stalker from a B-grade horror movie. The evolution of cyber threats has been a wild ride from quirky and quaint to cunning and cutthroat. Stay tuned and keep your antivirus handy because who knows what the next chapter in this digital saga will bring!

AI and ML to the Rescue in 2024

Fasten your seatbelts because 2024 looks like a sci-fi movie with AI and ML (Artificial Intelligence and Machine Learning) playing the lead roles in cybersecurity. Imagine cybersecurity systems with brains like Einstein and reflexes like a cat, learning and adapting to new threats faster than you can say "cyberattack." These AI gurus are set to become the superheroes of the digital realm, constantly one step ahead of the baddies and maybe even making a mean cup of virtual coffee while they're at it.

The IoT Invasion and Its Security Saga

By 2024, it was expected that there would be more IoT devices than people at a rock concert, around 41.6 billion, to be precise. Everything, from your toaster to your teddy bear, might have been connected to the Internet. This IoT invasion was turning our homes into a digital zoo, and keeping all these devices secure was like herding cybernetic cats. IoT security was set to become as crucial as locking your front door because nobody wanted their smart fridge going rogue and ordering a truckload of milk on its own.

Cloud Security - The New Guardians of the Galaxy

With cloud computing having become as common as a smartphone, by 2023, it was expected to handle 60% of all business workloads. This made cloud security the new guardian of our digital galaxy. It was like building a fortress in the sky to protect your virtual gold. As we floated more of our data into the cloud, ensuring its security became more crucial than ever, lest it rained down like confetti in the hands of cyber villains.

The Tightening Grip of Data Privacy Policies

Governments and regulatory bodies are expected to tighten the leash on data privacy policies as we continue to produce data faster than popcorn in a microwave. It's like having a digital Big Brother watching over us, ensuring our personal information isn't treated like a free-for-all buffet at a hacker's convention. Stricter policies mean businesses must be on their best behaviour when handling customer data or facing the music.

The Rising Tide of Cybercrime Costs and Cyber Insurance

Hold onto your wallets because the costs associated with cybercrime are soaring sky-high. This has businesses scrambling to get cyber insurance like it's the hottest ticket in town. Think of it as a safety net for when digital acrobats perform without a net. As cyber threats evolve, investing in cyber insurance is like having an umbrella in a downpour of digital threats – it might not stop the rain, but it'll keep you from getting soaked.

Quantum Computing - The New Kid on the Cyber Block

Lastly, let's talk about the new kid on the block - quantum computing. It's like the wildcard in a deck, capable of shaking up the cybersecurity world and cracking codes that would take traditional computers aeons. While it poses a significant threat to existing encryption methods, it's also the secret ingredient in creating new, quantum-resistant encryption recipes. Quantum computing in cybersecurity is like playing chess with a grandmaster; you've got to think several moves ahead or risk being checkmated.

Overall, cybersecurity is anticipated to remain a central concern in 2023 and beyond. To fortify against cyber-attacks, cybersecurity experts must remain vigilant and stay abreast of evolving trends as new technologies emerge.

Let's gain a deeper understanding of cybercrime with an intriguing case study:

Once upon a time, in the bustling cityscape of Mumbai, there lived a diligent and astute engineer named Samuel. Samuel, a quiet yet brilliant individual, worked for Techno Sphere, a cutting-edge tech company at the forefront of innovation. As a seasoned engineer, Samuel was entrusted with maintaining the integrity of the company's digital infrastructure.

One fateful Monday morning, as Samuel sipped his coffee and scanned through his emails, he stumbled upon an alert that sent shivers down his spine. The company's cybersecurity system had detected unusual activities, signalling a potential cyber threat. Determined to unravel this digital mystery, Samuel immediately dove into action.

He meticulously traced the anomaly, following a trail of encrypted breadcrumbs through the vast network of servers and firewalls. The clock ticked relentlessly as Samuel, fueled by determination and expertise, decrypted the malicious code that had stealthily infiltrated their systems.

He discovered a sophisticated cyber-attack aimed at siphoning sensitive data and exploiting vulnerabilities in the company's security protocols.

Samuel wasted no time. He swiftly implemented countermeasures, fortifying the company's defences and neutralising the threat. His technical prowess and quick thinking not only thwarted the cyber-attack but also prevented a potentially devastating data breach.

In a clandestine corner of the Internet, the cybercriminals retreated, frustrated by their thwarted efforts. Little did they know that Samuel, armed with his cybersecurity acumen, had turned the tide.

As the dust settled, Samuel presented his findings to the company's leadership. His thorough investigation and timely intervention not only saved sensitive data from falling into the wrong hands but also prevented a financial catastrophe. The potential loss of millions of dollars was averted, and the company's reputation remained untarnished.

Techno Sphere, recognising Samuel's invaluable contribution, applauded his dedication and expertise. Samuel became a cybersecurity hero, not just within the walls of Techno Sphere but also in the broader cybersecurity community. His story became a beacon of inspiration, emphasising the importance of vigilance and expertise in the ever-evolving landscape of cyber threats.

Thus, Samuel's quiet heroism underscored the crucial role of cybersecurity in the digital age, proving that sometimes, it takes just one determined engineer to safeguard a company's future and financial well-being.

The Domino Effect of Breaches:

Consider for a moment the aftermath of a cybersecurity breach for a startup. The consequences extend far beyond the immediate financial losses or regulatory penalties. The erosion of customer trust, damage to the brand reputation, and the disruption of business operations can have a cascading impact, potentially leading to irreparable harm.

In a landscape where startups often operate on slim margins and depend on investor confidence, a single cybersecurity incident can derail even the most promising ventures. Investors, customers, and partners alike scrutinise a startup's commitment to cybersecurity as a litmus test of its resilience and reliability.

While regulatory compliance is crucial to cybersecurity, startups must transcend the notion that meeting minimum standards is sufficient. Cybersecurity is not merely a box to check to satisfy regulatory bodies; it is a proactive strategy to fortify the foundations of a startup against an ever-evolving threat landscape.

A holistic approach to cybersecurity involves understanding that threats are dynamic and adapting security measures accordingly. Startups need to build a cybersecurity culture that touches every part of the organisation, making all employees aware and responsible. This change turns cybersecurity from a reactive approach into a proactive and essential part of the company's values.

As startups navigate the complexities of the digital ecosystem, cybersecurity should not be viewed as a necessary evil but rather as a strategic imperative. It represents an investment in the longevity and prosperity of the venture. Beyond safeguarding data, cybersecurity becomes a differentiator, a competitive advantage that instils confidence in stakeholders—be they investors, customers, or partners.

In conclusion, the cybersecurity imperative for startups is not a mere acknowledgement of risk; it is a commitment to resilience, reliability, and sustained success. By embracing cybersecurity as an integral part of the startup journey, entrepreneurs can confidently navigate the digital landscape, secure in the knowledge that they are not just safeguarding data but fortifying the essence of their innovative endeavours.

Navigating the Road Ahead: Crafting a Strategic Cybersecurity Roadmap

For tech startups, where innovation and speed are key, starting with cybersecurity is like exploring unknown territory. The ever-changing digital world needs a clear plan. This strategy makes cybersecurity easier to understand and guides you through each step. It's a manageable process, with intentional actions rather than a huge, difficult task.

The first point on the cybersecurity roadmap is understanding the unique digital landscape of your startup. No two startups are identical; similarly, their digital footprints differ significantly. Begin by conducting a comprehensive assessment of the types of data your startup handles. Is it customer information, proprietary algorithms, or sensitive market insights? Identifying these digital assets is foundational to tailoring an effective cybersecurity strategy.

Moreover, understanding the potential entry points for cyber threats is critical. In an interconnected world, startups often utilise a variety of digital platforms, cloud services, and collaborative tools. Recognising and mapping out these potential vulnerabilities is akin to marking the coordinates on your cybersecurity map, providing clarity on where to fortify your defences.

Assessing Risk Tolerance and Impact:

With a clearer understanding of your startup's digital landscape, the next step in crafting your cybersecurity roadmap involves assessing risk tolerance and potential impact. Not all risks are created equal, and neither are their consequences. Define your startup's risk tolerance—the level of risk your venture is willing to accept—and align it with the potential impact of various cyber threats.

This risk assessment serves as a compass, guiding you to prioritise security measures that align with your startup's unique risk profile. Are you handling sensitive customer data that demands a high level of protection? Or is the focus on safeguarding intellectual property that requires a different set of security measures? The answers to these questions develop your cybersecurity strategy, ensuring a tailored and efficient approach.

Establishing Foundational Security Policies:

As your journey progresses, you reach a pivotal point where the creation of foundational security policies becomes imperative. These policies are the guiding principles and the constitution of your startup's cybersecurity framework. They should be comprehensive, covering data protection, access controls, incident response procedures, and employee training.

Clear communication of these policies to all stakeholders, from C-suite executives to front-line employees, is essential. Building a culture of cybersecurity awareness within the organisation fosters a collective responsibility for digital security. This cultural shift transforms cybersecurity from a mere set of rules to an ingrained aspect of the organisational ethos.

Implementing Basic Security Measures:

With policies in place, the cybersecurity roadmap leads to implementing basic security measures. These are the foundational building blocks that fortify your startup against common cyber threats. Initiatives such as implementing multi-factor authentication, encrypting sensitive data, and regularly updating software and systems are akin to securing the perimeter of your digital fortress.

This phase includes both technical steps and educational efforts. Training employees on cybersecurity best practices, spotting phishing attempts, and using secure passwords builds a strong defence. Remember, your cybersecurity strength depends not just on technology but on your team's awareness and diligence.

Towards a Culture of Cybersecurity:

As you progress along the cybersecurity roadmap, a noteworthy transition occurs—the establishment of a culture of cybersecurity within your startup. This cultural shift involves more than just policies and procedures; it's about instilling a mindset where every team member views cybersecurity as an integral part of their role.

Encourage a proactive approach to cybersecurity, where employees are not just following protocols but actively identifying and reporting potential threats. Building this culture requires ongoing communication, training, and reinforcement. It transforms cybersecurity from a checklist item to an ethos, creating an environment where everyone understands their role in safeguarding the startup's digital assets.

Continuous Monitoring and Adaptation:

The cybersecurity journey is not a one-time expedition but an ongoing voyage. Your roadmap now involves continuous monitoring and adaptation to the ever-evolving threat landscape. Cyber threats are dynamic, and new vulnerabilities may emerge as your startup grows and adopts new technologies. Regular risk assessments, penetration testing, and staying abreast of industry trends are essential components of this phase.

As part of this continuous journey, fostering a mindset of adaptability is crucial. Flexibility in your cybersecurity strategy allows your startup to pivot and respond swiftly to emerging threats.

Remember, the goal is to secure data and fortify your startup's foundation for sustained success. With each intentional step, you build a more robust defence, fostering confidence among investors, customers, and partners. In this digital odyssey, your cybersecurity roadmap becomes the compass that guides your startup through uncharted waters, ensuring a resilient and secure voyage into the future.

Shifting Perspectives: From Necessity to Strategic Imperative:

Historically, cybersecurity has been perceived by some as a burdensome cost, a requisite checkbox to satisfy regulatory bodies. However, this perspective is an antiquated relic in the contemporary startup landscape. As startups navigate the complexities of the digital ecosystem, the understanding of cybersecurity must undergo a paradigm shift. It is no longer a necessary evil but a strategic imperative that plays a pivotal role in shaping the trajectory of a startup.

This shift in perspective involves recognising cybersecurity as an investment rather than an expenditure. Instead of viewing it solely as a means to mitigate risk, startups should see cybersecurity as an opportunity to fortify the longevity and prosperity of the venture.

Consider cybersecurity as a long-term investment that pays dividends in the form of sustained success and resilience. Startups are not just safeguarding data but preserving their reputation, customer trust, and the foundation on which their innovative ventures stand. The cost of a cybersecurity breach, both financially and reputationally, can far outweigh the investment in preventive measures.

By investing in robust cybersecurity practices, startups create a secure environment to innovate confidently. This security extends beyond the digital realm; it permeates the organisation's culture, instilling a sense of trust and reliability among stakeholders. Investors recognise the value of such investments, understanding that a startup with a fortified cybersecurity posture is better positioned for sustained growth.

Cybersecurity as a Competitive Differentiator:

In the competitive landscape of startups, where similar products or services often vie for attention, differentiation is vital. Cybersecurity, when strategically positioned, becomes a powerful differentiator. It is not just about meeting regulatory requirements; it is about surpassing them to establish a standard of excellence in safeguarding digital assets.

Roadmap for a SaaS-based Startup

Let's now look at a sample 3-month roadmap for a SaaS-based Startup.

Creating a detailed 3-month cybersecurity roadmap for a SaaS-based FinTech startup involves a series of strategic steps, each with specific sub-tasks, timelines, and responsible personnel. Given the sensitive nature of financial data and the regulatory requirements of the FinTech industry, this roadmap emphasises security and compliance.

Here's a proposed plan:

Month 1: Foundation and Assessment

Week 1: Kickoff and Team Formation

- **Sub-task:** Assemble a cybersecurity team.
- **Timeline:** 1 week.
- **Responsible Person**: CTO/V-CISO.

Week 2-3: Cybersecurity Training and Awareness

- **Sub-task**: Conduct company-wide cybersecurity training.
- **Timeline:** 2 weeks.
- **Responsible Person:** HR and Cybersecurity Team Lead.

Week 4: Risk Assessment and Compliance Review

- **Sub-task**: Perform a comprehensive risk assessment.
- **Timeline**: 1 week.
- **Responsible Person**: Cybersecurity Analysts.

Month 2: Implementation and Integration

Week 1-2: Implementing Basic Cybersecurity Controls

- **Sub-task:** Set up firewalls, antivirus software, and secure Wi-Fi networks.

- **Timeline:** 2 weeks.
- **Responsible Person**: IT Administrator.

Week 3: Secure Software Development Lifecycle (SDLC) Integration

- **Sub-task**: Integrate security practices into SDLC.
- **Timeline**: 1 week.
- The responsible person is the lead developer/Develops.

Week 4: Data Encryption and Access Control

- **Sub-task**: Encrypt sensitive data and implement robust access control.
- **Timeline**: 1 week.
- **Responsible Person**: Database Administrator/Security Engineer.

Month 3: Strengthening and Review

Week 1-2: Advanced Security Measures

- **Sub-task:** Deploy advanced security solutions (e.g., intrusion detection systems).
- **Timeline**: 2 weeks.
- **Responsible Person**: Cybersecurity Specialist.

Week 3: Incident Response Plan Development

- **Sub-task**: Develop and document an incident response plan.
- **Timeline**: 1 week.
- The responsible person is the CISO/Cybersecurity Team.

Week 4: Review and Audit

- **Sub-task**: Conduct an internal security audit and review the implemented measures.
- **Timeline:** 1 week.
- The responsible person is the internal auditor/cybersecurity team.

Ongoing: Continuous Monitoring and Improvement

- **Sub-task:** Establish ongoing monitoring of security systems and regular updates.
- **Timeline:** Continuous.
- **Responsible Person**: IT Support/Cybersecurity Analysts.

Each task should undergo close monitoring of progress and effectiveness, with adjustments made as necessary. Regular team meetings must be scheduled to ensure all tasks are on track and to address any challenges that arise. This roadmap is intentionally designed to be flexible, allowing for adjustments based on emerging threats and changing regulatory requirements in the FinTech sector.

Conclusion

As we close this chapter, it's important to note that the journey of cybersecurity is not just about technical safeguards and reactive measures. The next chapter is dedicated to a critical aspect of this journey: building robust compliance and governance frameworks.

Chapter 2 will explore how to weave these frameworks into the fabric of your startup's operations. We'll delve into the intricacies of aligning with industry standards and regulatory requirements and how to establish governance structures that meet legal obligations and foster a culture of security and responsibility.

Chapter - 2

Orchestrating Cybersecurity GOvernance, Risk, And COmpliance

Overview

"GRC is a capability that enables an organization to reliably achieve objectives while addressing uncertainty and acting with integrity."

- Michael Rasmussen (Chief GRC Pundit)

As we kick off Chapter 2, let's meet Sam - a character whose journey into the labyrinth of compliance and Governance starts with a twist that could make even a seasoned comedian chuckle. Picture this:

- Sam beaming with pride and ambition
- Steps into his new role as a security lead at a fintech company

However, his bubble of euphoria quickly bursts when the CTO, sporting a poker champion's straight face, drops a bombshell of a task on him: Implement ISO 27001 and navigate through a jungle of banking regulations with compliance. Sam, who previously thought ISO was a type of camera setting and banking regulations were suggestions rather than laws, found himself in a dizzying world of compliance acronyms and legalese.

Overwhelmed and slightly panicked, he dived headfirst into a sea of documents and consultations, hoping to find the lifebuoy of understanding in the vast ocean of standards and regulations. Night after night, he pored over guidelines that seemed to be written in an alien language and attended meetings with experts who often spoke in riddles. It was like trying to solve a Rubik's Cube in the dark. Nevertheless, as we'll see, Sam's journey from a bewildered novice to a confident maestro of compliance and Governance is a tale of perseverance and a humorous and enlightening adventure into the world of cybersecurity standards. So, buckle up and prepare for a ride filled with unexpected twists, turns, and maybe even a few laughs!

Objectives

After studying this chapter, you will understand:

- Basics of Governance, Risk, and Compliance (GRC)
- Understanding Governance in Cybersecurity
- Why is Risk Management Crucial for Start-ups?
- Importance of GRC for Startups?
- Steps to Implement GRC
- Popular GRC tools

Governance, Risk, and Compliance (GRC)

Have you heard the terms ' Governance,' 'Risk,' and 'Compliance' (GRC) and wondered what they're all about? It may sound like a trio of business superheroes or a complex board game with too many rules. If you're nodding your head, you're not alone. Like Sam, our bewildered security lead, you might feel like you're venturing into a maze filled with corporate jargon and intricate concepts. But fear not! Understanding GRC is crucial for your business and is more manageable than it seems.

Are you curious to unravel the mysteries of GRC and discover how it can be a game-changer for your startup? If your answer is a resounding 'Yes!', you're in for an enlightening journey. Let's dive into the world of GRC together and explore how mastering these concepts can bolster your company's security posture, ensure compliance with regulations, and manage risks effectively.

In cybersecurity, Governance, Risk, and Compliance (GRC) is the cornerstone for steering an organisation through the complexities of the digital world. Imagine GRC as the captain of a ship, navigating the vast seas of business operations, where Governance stands at the helm, risk management scans the horizon for potential storms, and compliance ensures the ship adheres to the maritime laws of the business world. This integrated approach is more than just following rules; it's about aligning your organisation's cybersecurity strategies with its fundamental values, objectives, and goals.

GRC solutions are the instruments and maps that guide this journey. They provide organisations with the means to track and remain compliant with relevant laws and regulations, identify and mitigate risks, and enhance operational efficiency. Through these means, GRC becomes an indispensable part of maintaining a secure, efficient, and law-abiding enterprise in the ever-evolving landscape of cybersecurity.

Let's examine the terms Governance, risk management, and compliance individually. Understanding the fundamentals of Governance, risk management, and compliance will help you protect your business and lead it to success:

Understanding Governance in Cybersecurity

Cybersecurity governance is not just a set of rules; it's a strategic orchestration that integrates deeply with an organisation's operations, especially in a startup. Governance, being the captain of your cyber ship, helps steer the startup away from the turbulent waters of cyber threats and attacks. It involves crafting a cybersecurity strategy in harmony with the startup's operational rhythm, defining how much risk the startup will take (its risk appetite), creating accountability frameworks, and deciding who calls the shots in security-related decisions. Effective Governance ensures that all cybersecurity efforts are in lockstep with the startup's strategic objectives, helping to identify and tackle potential risks while ensuring the organisation meets its key goals.

The Role of Risk Management

Risk management in cybersecurity is like having a seasoned navigator on board. It's an all-encompassing process involving three main components: risk assessment, management, and communication.

Why is Risk Management Crucial for Startups?

- **Adapting to a Rapidly Changing Tech Landscape**: Startups, especially in technology, navigate through ever-changing waters. Effective risk management helps them foresee and prepare for these shifts, staying ahead.

- **Navigating Uncertainty**: In the early stages, startups often sail through uncertain and unpredictable seas. Risk management helps chart a course through these challenges by identifying potential risks and preparing contingency plans.
- **Boosting Investor Confidence**: Investors are the wind in a startup's sails. Showing a solid approach to managing risks can strengthen investor trust, showing that the startup is a worthy vessel to board.
- **Compliance with Laws and Regulations**: The regulatory sea is vast and complex. Risk management ensures that startups remain compliant, avoiding the whirlpools of legal and regulatory troubles.
- **Safeguarding Reputation and Brand**: For startups, reputation is their flag. Risk management helps protect this flag from being tarnished by potential risks that could damage its image.

Compliance: The Anchor of GRC

Compliance in GRC acts as the anchor, ensuring that the organisation doesn't drift away from legal and regulatory requirements. It's about understanding and abiding by relevant laws and regulations and ensuring everyone in the organisation is on the same page. Compliance helps safeguard assets, reduce risks, and maintain the startup's standing in the regulatory landscape. It involves regular monitoring, assessment, and management of the organisation's activities to ensure they align with both internal standards and external legal requirements.

In essence, GRC in cybersecurity for a startup is like sailing a ship with Governance at the helm, risk management as the navigator, and compliance as the anchor, ensuring a safe and fruitful voyage in the dynamic seas of the digital world.

Importance of GRC for Startups?

Why does your organisation need GRC?

GRC helps to ensure that the business is well-managed, risks are minimised, and the company complies with applicable laws and regulations. GRC also helps to ensure operational efficiency and provides a foundation for effective decision-making.

By having a system to manage Governance, risk, and compliance, a startup can ensure that it is properly organised and that its operations are running smoothly. It can help to protect the company from potential legal issues or financial losses due to non-compliance or mismanagement.

If adequately implemented, GRC policies, practices, and software offer the following benefits:

- Reduced costs; improved leadership effectiveness across all aspects of governance; increased visibility into risks, threats, and vulnerabilities;
- Ongoing compliance with required standards and regulations;
- Protection against unfavourable internal audits, financial penalties, and litigation;
- Reduction in risk across the entire organisation, including business, financial, operational, and security risks.

GRC can be a daunting task for startups, as it requires significant resources and expertise. While GRC can help protect a startup from legal and financial risks, it can also be costly, especially if it needs more resources to implement GRC properly. Additionally, the startup may need to hire a consultant to help them understand their GRC needs and develop an effective plan.

Understanding the potential risks and costs

When a startup is considering implementing a Governance, Risk, and Compliance (GRC) program, it must consider its potential risks and costs. GRC programs can be expensive, as they require resources to manage, track, and report on the various elements of the program.

This could lead to costly mistakes or even legal action. Furthermore, implementing a GRC program can require significant staff training, which can add to the cost. Finally, startups must also consider the potential risks associated with the data they are collecting, such as data loss, theft, or misuse.

To implement an effective governance risk and compliance, it is essential to get buy-in structure a discussion with investors as to the appropriateness of their management of cyber security risk; engage with investors to help them compare and contrast differing approaches to the management of cyber security risk, and facilitate a discussion as to what would be appropriate for companies to report publicly concerning cyber security.

Navigating the GRC landscape in a startup environment presents its own set of unique challenges. Firstly, startups often grapple with resource constraints; they typically don't have the luxury of large teams or deep pockets to manage GRC processes comprehensively. This scarcity of resources often means that startups need help to allocate sufficient funds for robust GRC systems or to bring on board specialised personnel.

Moreover, there often needs to be more technical know-how. Many startups may find themselves in murky waters when fully grasping the intricacies of GRC requirements. The challenge is not just in the implementation but also in the ongoing development and maintenance of effective GRC policies. This is compounded by the need to understand the startup's specific risk profile, which requires a nuanced approach to identify and mitigate potential risks.

Additionally, the pace and scale of change in startups can make GRC a moving target. The startup world moves quickly, and keeping GRC processes aligned with rapid growth and change is no small feat. This is further complicated because many startups are breaking new ground in uncharted territories, where standard GRC procedures may not readily apply or may need significant adaptation.

Lastly, there's the challenge of experience - or the lack thereof. Many startups are venturing into GRC for the first time and may need to possess the necessary experience or knowledge for effective implementation. The option to hire external consultants or specialists to fill this gap is often constrained by budget limitations, leaving startups to navigate these complex waters with limited guidance.

While GRC is critical for startups, it's a path fraught with challenges related to resources, expertise, and the dynamic nature of startup ecosystems. Addressing these challenges requires a strategic, adaptable approach, often calling for innovative solutions tailored to the unique environment of startups.

Steps to Implement GRC

Risk management is a vital cog in cybersecurity, particularly for SMEs and startups, where the impact of cyber threats can be disproportionately severe. Cybersecurity risk management is about identifying, analysing, and mitigating risks associated with digital assets and operations. This process begins with risk identification, recognising potential threats and vulnerabilities that could adversely affect the organisation. Once these risks are identified, they are carefully analysed to assess their potential impact and likelihood. This analysis helps prioritise risks based on their severity and the probability of their occurrence, enabling organisations to allocate their resources more effectively.

The methodologies employed in cybersecurity risk management are diverse and must be adapted to the specific context of the business. One common approach is using risk matrices or heat maps that visually represent the severity and likelihood of various risks, aiding in better decision-making. Another critical aspect is the implementation of risk mitigation strategies. These can range from technical solutions, like firewalls and encryption, to administrative measures, like policy changes and staff training. The goal is to reduce the risk to an acceptable level, understanding that not all risks can be eliminated.

For SMEs and startups, an effective risk management strategy is not just a one-time task but an ongoing process. It involves regularly monitoring and re-evaluating risks and keeping abreast of the evolving cybersecurity landscape. This continuous process ensures that the organisation can adapt to new threats, technologies, and business changes, maintaining a robust defence against potential cyber-attacks. In essence, mastering the fundamentals of risk management is critical for these smaller businesses to navigate the digital world securely and confidently.

Define Your Risks

When successfully implementing GRC, one of the most important steps is to define your risks. This means identifying and assessing the potential risks associated with your organisation and its operations. A risk assessment should identify the sources, the likelihood of occurrence, the potential impact, and the controls necessary to mitigate or reduce the risk.

There are several types of cybersecurity risk – it's essential to carry out a detailed risk assessment of your organisation to understand the risk landscape to your organisation; the risk will depend upon your geography and industry. However, below are some of the generic and common risks for any startup.

Some common cybersecurity risks to startups include:

- **Phishing attacks**: Hackers use phishing emails to trick employees into divulging sensitive information or clicking on malicious links, which can compromise the entire network.
- **Malware**: Malware is software designed to disrupt, damage, or gain unauthorised access to a computer system. Startups may not have adequate anti-malware software or may not keep their software updated, making them vulnerable to malware attacks.
- **Insider threats**: Employees or contractors may intentionally or unintentionally compromise the startup's data by stealing sensitive information or inadvertently introducing vulnerability into the network.
- **Third-party risks**: Startups may rely on third-party vendors for various services, such as hosting or payment processing, which can expose the startup to additional security risks.
- **Weak passwords**: Weak or easily guessable passwords can be easily cracked by attackers, leaving the startup's sensitive information vulnerable to compromise. A cyber risk assessment is crucial in identifying and mitigating cybersecurity risks. The following are some steps to carry out a cyber risk assessment:
- **Identify the assets**: Identify all the assets within the organisation that need to be protected, such as hardware, software, data, and intellectual property.
- **Identify the potential threats**: Identify potential threats that could impact the assets. Threats could include cyber-attacks, malware infections, data breaches, insider threats, and natural

disasters.

- **Determine the likelihood of the threat**: Analyse each identified threat's likelihood and potential impact on the organisation. This can be done by assessing the likelihood of the threat occurring and the severity of its impact.
- **Evaluate current security measures**: Evaluate the current security measures to protect the assets. This can include reviewing policies, procedures, and technologies currently in use.
- **Identify vulnerabilities**: Identify any vulnerabilities that a cyber attacker could exploit. This can include outdated software, weak passwords, and a lack of employee training.
- **Prioritise risks**: Prioritise the identified risks based on the likelihood and potential impact on the organisation.
- **Develop a risk mitigation plan**: Develop a plan to mitigate the identified risks, including specific measures to address each risk. This plan may include implementing new security controls, updating existing policies and procedures, and providing employee training.
- **Implement and monitor**: Implement the risk mitigation plan and monitor the effectiveness of the measures. Ongoing monitoring and regular updates to the risk assessment are critical to ensure that new threats are identified and addressed promptly.

In summary, a cyber risk assessment involves identifying and prioritising potential threats to the organisation's assets and developing a plan to mitigate those risks. This process should be carried out regularly to protect the organisation's sensitive information and assets.

Additionally, it is essential to consider the cost of implementing the risk management strategy and its potential benefits of doing so. Once the risks have been identified and assessed, it is vital to develop a comprehensive risk management strategy that includes policies, procedures, and controls to address the identified risks.

Identify Your Audience

Knowing who is affected by the GRC program and how they will be impacted is essential to understanding how to implement the program best. Before starting the GRC implementation process, it is crucial to identify who will be involved in the program. This could include stakeholders, customers, employees, and other interested parties.

Once you have identified who will be affected by the GRC program, you can determine the best way to communicate the program's goals and objectives to those involved. It would be best if you also considered their input and feedback when making decisions about the program.

Develop Your Policies and Procedures

The next step is to develop policies and procedures that outline the organisation's expectations for managing risk, compliance, and governance. This should include a clear definition of roles and responsibilities, a process for identifying and assessing risks, and a plan for responding to and mitigating those risks. (We can plug in the Sprinto tool for creating automated policies.)

Developing policies and procedures is an essential aspect of establishing a solid foundation for a startup. Here are some steps to follow when developing policies and procedures:

- **Identify the areas that require policies and procedures:** Identify the areas of the startup that require policies and procedures. For example, these may include HR policies, IT policies, data privacy policies, safety policies, and financial policies.

- **Define each policy's scope and objectives**: Clearly define each policy's scope and objectives, ensuring that it addresses the specific risks and challenges faced by the startup.

- **Involve relevant stakeholders**: Involve relevant stakeholders, including employees, managers, and subject matter experts, in the policy development process. This can help ensure that the policies are relevant, practical, and effective.

- **Draft the policies and procedures**: Draft the policies and procedures, ensuring that they are clear, concise, and easy to understand. Use simple language and avoid technical jargon as much as possible.
- **Review and refine**: Review the policies and procedures regularly, making necessary changes to ensure that they remain relevant and practical. Get feedback from employees and stakeholders to ensure that the policies are being implemented effectively and that they address any new risks or challenges that may arise.
- **Communicate and train**: Communicate the policies and procedures to all employees and ensure they are trained to implement them effectively. This can include providing training sessions, posting the policies on the company intranet, and providing regular reminders about the policies and procedures.

How can the right tools help your GRC strategy?

Having the right tools for your GRC strategy can be the difference between success and failure. The right tools help to ensure that all of the necessary steps are taken to ensure compliance with laws and regulations and provide a framework for managing risk.

A GRC platform can provide a centralised repository for all of the necessary documents, policies, and procedures, making it easier for stakeholders to access the information they need. Additionally, GRC tools can help automate processes, such as risk assessments, to ensure they are done quickly and accurately. The right tools can provide real-time monitoring and reporting capabilities to help identify potential issues before they become a problem.

While there are many tools and standards in the market, my recommendation is to focus on implementing the ISO 27001 standard with the help of ManageEngine's IT management and security solutions. These solutions enable startups to meet several of the IT-related controls needed for ISO 27001 compliance across each of the four control categories given in the standard.

- **Organisation controls:** Create and maintain IT asset and network inventory, enforce access control policies, leverage threat intelligence and real-time security monitoring, and ensure regular backups for disaster recovery.

- **People control:** Ensure secure remote access for remote employees, simplify incident reporting, and automate incident triaging and response.

- **Physical controls:** Classify, manage, and monitor devices throughout their lifecycles, and ensure all corporate data is wiped before device disposal.

- **Technological controls:** Ensure end-to-end protection for the organisation's IT infrastructure through access management and authentication, endpoint management, data loss prevention, network monitoring, and security monitoring and automation.

Key products: Endpoint Central, ServiceDesk Plus, Log360, AD360, Identity360, PAM360, OpManager Plus, Site24x7.

Visit www.manageengine.com/iso-27001 to know more.

Identity and Access Management Solutions from ManageEngine: As startups scale, managing user access across cloud and on-premise applications becomes increasingly complex. Identity and Access Management (IAM) ensures that the right individuals have the right access to the right resources, at the right time—and for the right reasons.

ManageEngine's identity and access management (IAM) solutions helps startups securely manage their digital identities and build a solid security foundation to scale confidently, stay audit-ready, and deliver seamless, fortified user experiences.

- **Identity life cycle management:** Automate provisioning, deprovisioning, and manage access rights across platforms to ensure timely, compliant access control for employees, contractors, and more.

- **User authentication:** Enforce risk-based adaptive authentication and boost identity security with adaptive MFA, SSO, strong password policies, remote work enablement.

- **Granular role-based access control:** Implement role-based access control to minimise risk, enforce the least privilege principle, provide precise stakeholder access, and distribute privileged duties safely.
- **Privilege elevation and delegation management:** Assign just-in-time controls for domain accounts and provision higher privileges only when needed by users.
- **Behaviour analytics:** Detect, investigate, and mitigate threats, such as malicious logins, lateral movement, malware attacks, and privilege abuse, with ML-based user behaviour analytics.
- **Real-time auditing**: Receive audit reports on privileged user activity, insider threat detection, and root cause analysis. Monitor and be notified about logon activity and ACL or password changes.

Key ManageEngine products: AD360, Identity360 and PAM360

Visit www.manageengine.com/iam to know more.

There are several open-source tools you can explore, which are as follows-

Open-Audit: It is a powerful GRC tool that helps organisations track and manage their IT assets. It provides an automated way to collect detailed information about hardware, software, and network configurations. This information can be used to identify potential security risks, identify non-compliant systems, and enable organisations to meet compliance requirements.

OSSIM: OSSIM, or Open-Source Security Information Management, is a powerful GRC tool that helps organisations protect their networks and data. It is an open-source security platform that provides comprehensive tools for managing security risks and compliance. OSSIM provides real-time threat detection and incident response capabilities, as well as continuous monitoring and reporting.

Open Escape: It is a powerful open-source GRC tool that helps organisations automate the assessment and management of their IT infrastructure. This tool provides an integrated set of capabilities that enable organisations to quickly and accurately evaluate the security posture of their systems, identify vulnerabilities, and remediate them.

Tripwire: It is a comprehensive GRC tool that allows businesses to identify and monitor changes in IT systems, networks, and applications. It helps organisations proactively detect, investigate, and respond to security incidents. Tripwire's features include vulnerability assessment, file integrity monitoring, configuration management, and log management.

Open DLP: Open DLP is a powerful open-source GRC tool that helps organisations detect and protect against data leakage. It is a comprehensive, open-source data loss prevention (DLP) platform that allows organisations to quickly and easily detect, monitor, and protect sensitive data. Open DLP allows organisations to quickly scan their systems for sensitive data, such as credit card numbers, social security numbers, and other personally identifiable information.

Effective GRC (Governance, Risk, and Compliance) planning is a multifaceted endeavour that requires the active participation of various stakeholders within an organisation. At the helm, executive management is pivotal in shaping GRC's overarching vision and strategy. Their involvement is crucial in aligning GRC initiatives with the organisation's goals and objectives. On the ground, operational management takes the baton, ensuring the day-to-day execution and implementation of these strategies.

A key player in the GRC framework is the IT department, including roles such as DevOps, engineering heads, and the CTO. These individuals safeguard the security and privacy of the organisation's systems and data. Parallelly, the legal team is indispensable in navigating the complex waters of compliance, ensuring that all GRC activities adhere to relevant laws and regulations.

Another vital contributor is the internal audit function. Their role is to provide objective assurance on the effectiveness and efficiency of GRC processes, offering a critical evaluation of whether these initiatives are meeting their intended objectives.

Moreover, the board of directors holds a strategic position in GRC planning. They are responsible for setting the overall direction and providing oversight for GRC implementation. Their involvement ensures that GRC efforts are aligned with the organisational strategy and receive the necessary oversight and support at the highest level.

In the grand scheme of things, GRC is a tapestry woven from various threads – information security, governance, risk management, and compliance. The seamless integration of these elements is essential to safeguard the confidentiality, integrity, and availability of sensitive information and ensure compliance with applicable regulatory

requirements. This collaborative approach among diverse stakeholders is fundamental to creating a robust and resilient GRC framework.

With so many laws and regulations, and compliance requirements, it often needs clarification on where to start. There comes a framework to help us in this journey.

Frameworks are important in information security because they provide a structured approach to managing information security risks. They define a set of best practices, standards, and guidelines that organisations can follow to ensure that their information security program is effective and efficient. Frameworks provide a comprehensive approach to information security, covering all aspects of information security, including people, processes, and technology.

What are Information Security Standards and Frameworks?

Information security standards and frameworks provide organisations with the necessary guidelines for protecting their data and systems from unauthorised access, misuse, and manipulation. These standards and frameworks help businesses develop robust security measures to protect their IT infrastructure, applications, and digital assets from malicious attacks.

Regarding information security, having an adequate security standard or framework can be the difference between success and failure. These standards and frameworks aim to ensure that businesses have adequate security measures to protect their information technology assets from threats. These standards also help organisations comply with industry regulations, including the GDPR and HIPAA, and mitigate data loss and unauthorized access risks.

What are the types of Security Standards and Frameworks?

Security standards come in various forms, each of which is designed to provide guidance and protection for an organisation's data and systems. The most common types of security standards include:

- **ISO/IEC 27001**

The ISO/IEC 27001 Security Standard is an information security management system (ISMS) standard created by ISO and IEC. This standard provides an overarching framework for organisations to develop, implement, maintain, and continually improve their security systems.

It is based on a risk management approach, which requires organisations to assess their security risks and take appropriate steps to prevent, detect, and respond to security threats. The standard promotes a security culture, encouraging organisations to consider security aspects in all operations. The standard's requirements include establishing security policies, procedures, and controls, as well as selecting, implementing, and assessing these controls.

Getting ISO 27001 certification is a process that involves several steps. Here are the general steps you can take to get ISO 27001 certification:

Conduct a gap analysis: Conduct a gap analysis to identify the areas in your organisation that need to be improved to meet ISO 27001 requirements. This analysis will help you identify the gaps between your current information security practices and ISO 27001 standards.

Develop an information security management system (ISMS): Develop and implement an ISMS that meets the requirements of ISO 27001. This includes identifying and managing risks, defining policies and procedures, establishing security controls, and monitoring and reviewing the system.

Conduct internal audits: Conduct internal audits to ensure that your ISMS is effective and compliant with ISO 27001 standards. These audits will help you identify areas that need to be improved before the certification audit.

Choose a certification body: Choose a certification body accredited by the International Accreditation Forum (IAF) to conduct the certification audit.

Certification audit: The certification body will conduct a certification audit to verify that your ISMS meets ISO 27001 standards. This audit will include a document review, interviews with employees, and an assessment of your information security controls.

Corrective actions: If any non-conformities are identified during the certification audit, you must take corrective actions to address them.

Certification: If your ISMS is found to comply with ISO 27001 standards, the certification body will issue you an ISO 27001 certificate.

Surveillance audits: After certification, you must undergo periodic surveillance audits to ensure your ISMS complies with ISO 27001 standards.

Several open-source tools are available to automate various aspects of the ISO 27001 compliance process. Some popular open-source options include:

Open-Audit: This tool can be used to conduct automated inventory management and asset tracking, which is vital for identifying and assessing potential security risks.

Nessus: This tool can be used to conduct automated vulnerability scanning and penetration testing, which is essential for identifying and addressing potential security vulnerabilities.

OSSIM: This is a security information and event management (SIEM) tool that can be used to collect, analyse, and respond to security-related data from various sources.

Snort: This is an open-source intrusion detection and prevention system (IDS/IPS) that can be used to detect and respond to potential security threats in real-time.

OSSEC: This is an open-source host-based intrusion detection system (HIDS) that can be used to detect and respond to potential security threats on individual hosts.

OpenSCAP: This tool can be used to automate the process of auditing systems for compliance with various security standards, including ISO 27001.

The ISO27001 standard documentation toolkit contains templates and guidance for implementing and maintaining an ISMS.

Implementing ISO 27001, an international standard for information security management systems (ISMS), is a significant undertaking for a FinTech startup. The process demands meticulous planning, resource allocation, and a clear timeline. Here's a detailed plan for the implementation:

Phase 1: Preparation and Planning (1 Month)

Week 1-2: Initial Assessment and Gap Analysis

- Conduct a thorough assessment of current security practices against ISO 27001 standards.
- Identify gaps and areas for improvement.

Week 3: Assembling the Project Team

- Form a cross-functional team involving members from IT, legal, operations, and senior management.

Week 4: Training and Awareness

- Arrange training for the team on ISO 27001 requirements.
- Increase company-wide awareness of the upcoming changes.

Phase 2: Development of ISMS (2 Months)

Month 1: Risk Assessment and Management

- Conduct a detailed risk assessment.
- Develop a risk treatment plan.

Month 2: Documentation

- Develop the ISMS policy and objectives.
- Document control procedures, security policies, and operating procedures.

Phase 3: Implementation (2 Months)

Month 1: Control Implementation and Training

- Implement the necessary controls as per the risk treatment plan.
- Conduct training sessions for employees on new policies and procedures.

Month 2: Review and Internal Audit

- Regularly review the implementation process for any issues.
- Perform an internal audit to check compliance with ISO 27001 standards.

Phase 4: Certification Audit (1 Month)

Week 1-2: Pre-Certification Audit

- Conduct a pre-certification audit to ensure readiness for the official audit.

Week 3-4: Certification Audit

- Undergo an accredited external body's official ISO 27001 certification audit.
- Address any non-conformities identified by the auditors.

Phase 5: Post-Certification Activities (Ongoing)

Continuous Improvement

- Regularly update and improve the ISMS in line with business changes and feedback.
- Schedule annual surveillance audits to maintain the certification.

This roadmap spans approximately six months, with additional time for continuous improvement post-certification. It's important to note that timelines can vary based on the startup's size, complexity, and existing maturity level in information security practices. Regular communication, management support, and employee engagement are critical factors for a successful ISO 27001 implementation.

- **NIST**

The National Institute of Standards and Technology (NIST) Security Standard is a set of guidelines for organisations and individuals regarding cybersecurity. It provides a comprehensive framework of security controls, processes, and procedures that can be implemented to reduce risk and create a more secure environment.

The standard applies to all types of organisations, from small businesses to large enterprises, and can be used to enhance existing security measures or to build new ones. The goal of the standard is to help organisations protect their data, networks, systems, and applications from malicious actors.

Implement the NIST Cybersecurity Framework with ManageEngine.

Visit www.manageengine.com/nist-cybersecurity-framework.html to know more.

- **PCI DSS**

Payment Card Industry Data Security Standard (PCI DSS) is a comprehensive security framework to shield cardholder data and ensure that the processing of credit card transactions is safe and secure.

PCI DSS provides a set of requirements for organisations that store, process, or transmit cardholder data to safeguard against data breaches and other security vulnerabilities. The framework includes a variety of security controls, including technical, physical, and organisational requirements.

Technical controls cover encryption, authentication, access control, logging, and monitoring. Physical controls, such as security guards, video surveillance, and locks, help to protect physical access to cardholder data.

Comply with PCI DSS using ManageEngine solutions.

Visit www.manageengine.com/pci-dss-compliance-solutions to know more.

What is SOC 2?

SOC 2 (Service Organisation Control 2) is an auditing procedure designed to ensure that service providers securely manage data to protect the interests and privacy of their clients. Developed by the American Institute of CPAs (AICPA), SOC 2 is specifically intended for technology and cloud computing organisations. It focuses on five "trust service principles": security, availability, processing integrity, confidentiality, and privacy.

What is SOC 2 Type 2?

There are two types of SOCS 2 reports, including Type 1 and Type 2. SOC 2 Type 1 describes a vendor's systems and whether their design is suitable to meet relevant trust principles. SOC 2 Type 2 details the operational effectiveness of those systems over a defined period, typically at least six months. This means SOC 2 Type 2 is more thorough as it includes the auditor's opinion on the effectiveness of the controls during the review period.

Importance of SOC 2 Type 2 for a FinTech Company

For a FinTech company, achieving SOC 2 Type 2 compliance is crucial as it assures clients and stakeholders that the company adheres to high standards in handling and securing data. Given the sensitive nature of financial data, SOC 2 Type 2 compliance can significantly enhance a FinTech company's credibility and trustworthiness. It also helps comply with regulatory requirements and can give a competitive edge in the market.

Implementation Plan for SOC 2 Type 2 Compliance

Phase 1: Preparation (1-2 Months)

- **Gap Analysis and Planning**: Conduct a gap analysis to understand current practices versus SOC 2 requirements. Develop a roadmap for compliance.
- **Assemble a Compliance Team**: Form a team responsible for SOC 2 compliance, involving members from IT, security, legal, and operations.

Phase 2: Development and Documentation (2-3 Months)

- **Policy and Procedure Development**: Develop and document policies and procedures that address the five trust service principles.
- **Risk Assessment**: Conduct a thorough risk assessment to identify and mitigate data security and privacy risks.

Phase 3: Implementation (3-4 Months)

- **Implement Controls**: Implement the necessary controls as per the developed policies. This includes IT controls, security measures, and process changes.
- **Employee Training**: Conduct training sessions for employees on new policies, procedures, and their roles in compliance.

Phase 4: Internal Audit (1-2 Months)

Conduct Internal Audit: Before the official audit, perform an internal audit to ensure all controls work effectively as per SOC 2 requirements.

Phase 5: External Audit and Certification (2-3 Months)

- **Engage with an Auditor:** Engage with a third-party auditing firm specialising in SOC 2 audits.
- **Official SOC 2 Type 2 Audit:** Undergo the official SOC 2 Type 2 audit. The auditor will assess the effectiveness of controls over a period (at least six months).

Phase 6: Continuous Compliance and Improvement (Ongoing)

- **Monitoring and Updating Controls:** Regularly monitor and update the controls as per the changing business environment and feedback.
- **Annual Audits:** Conduct annual audits to maintain SOC 2 Type 2 compliance.

Achieving SOC 2 Type 2 compliance is a detailed and ongoing process that requires commitment and involvement from various departments within a FinTech company. Regular updates and continuous monitoring are crucial for maintaining compliance and ensuring data security and privacy.

- **HIPAA**

The Health Insurance Portability and Accountability Act (HIPAA) Security Rule is a federal law that establishes a framework of administrative, physical, and technical safeguards to protect electronic protected health information (ePHI). This framework is essential to ensure the security and confidentiality of all ePHI, its integrity and availability.

The Security Rule also gives individuals the right to access and control their ePHI.

To become HIPAA compliant, you need to take the following steps:

- **Learn about HIPAA regulations:** Review the HIPAA Privacy and Security Rules to understand the requirements for safeguarding PHI.
- **Conduct a risk analysis**: Perform a risk analysis to identify potential security risks to PHI and establish appropriate safeguards.
- **Develop policies and procedures**: Develop and implement policies and procedures that address the HIPAA Privacy and Security Rules requirements.
- **Train employees**: Ensure that all PHI employees receive HIPAA training covering the organisation's policies and procedures.
- **Perform regular audits**: Regularly audit the organisation's systems and processes to ensure ongoing compliance with HIPAA regulations.
- **Document compliance efforts**: Document all compliance efforts, including policies and procedures, risk analyses, training, and audits.
- **Stay up to date**: Keep up with any changes to HIPAA regulations and adjust your compliance efforts accordingly.

While there is no formal certification process for HIPAA compliance, you can seek guidance from a qualified HIPAA compliance consultant or organization to help you navigate the regulations and develop an effective compliance program.

Comply with HIPAA using ManageEngine solutions.

Visit https://www.manageengine.com/hipaa-compliance.html to know more.

- **COBIT**

COBIT is an information security framework developed by the Information Systems Audit and Control Association (ISACA). It stands for Control Objectives for Information and Related Technology and provides a comprehensive set of best practices for managing and governing information technology (IT) systems. COBIT is designed to help organisations achieve their IT-related goals by providing a set of processes, controls, and metrics to ensure the security and reliability of IT systems.

It also helps organisations assess the effectiveness of their IT security measures and identify areas of improvement. COBIT includes:

Processes for managing IT risks.

Ensuring compliance with applicable laws and regulations. Setting up a framework for IT governance.

- **CIS Controls**

CIS Controls are security standards developed by the Centre for Internet Security (CIS) to help organisations protect their critical assets and systems. These standards provide a comprehensive, prioritised list of actionable steps organisations can take to protect their networks and data.

The standards are divided into 20 categories, each containing five controls. These controls are designed to address the most common cyber threats and provide a framework for organisations to build their security program. CIS Controls are widely used by organisations of all sizes, from small businesses to large enterprises, as they effectively protect against the most common cyber threats.

Comply with CIS Controls using ManageEngine solutions.

Visit www.manageengine.com/cis-critical-security-controls to know more.

- **CERT-IN Compliance**

CERT-In (Indian Computer Emergency Response Team) is a government-mandated organisation in India responsible for protecting the country's critical information infrastructure from cyber threats. To comply with CERT-In, an organisation must go through a formal process. This typically includes the following steps:

- Understand the requirements of CERT-In and determine how the organisation's current information security practices align with those requirements.
- Develop and implement a comprehensive information security program that meets the requirements of CERT-In. This program should include policies, procedures, and controls for information security, such as risk management, incident management, and security awareness training.
- Conduct internal assessments and audits to verify compliance with CERT-In standards.
- Obtain certification from an accredited certification body by undergoing an independent assessment, which may include on-site audits.
- Maintain compliance with CERT-In by conducting ongoing monitoring and periodic recertification.
- Report any cyber incidents to CERT-In as per the incident reporting guidelines.

It is recommended that you seek guidance from a professional consultant or certification body to help you through the process.

From a cybersecurity perspective, a fintech company operating in India must comply with several regulatory requirements to protect the sensitive financial data. Some of these requirements include:

- **Privacy**

Data privacy refers to protecting personal information that is collected, processed, stored, and shared by organisations. It includes the right of individuals to control how their personal information is collected, used, and shared by others.

There are several laws governing data privacy in various countries. Here are some examples:

1. **United States**: The primary law governing data privacy in the United States is the California Consumer Privacy Act (CCPA), which went

into effect in 2020. The CCPA requires businesses that collect, use, or sell personal information of California residents to provide certain rights to those residents, including the right to know what information is being collected, the right to request deletion of that information and the right to opt out of the sale of that information.

2. **European Union**: The General Data Protection Regulation (GDPR) is the primary law governing data privacy in the European Union (EU). The GDPR went into effect in 2018 and requires businesses that collect, use, or process personal information of EU residents to provide certain rights to those residents, including the right to access their data, the right to rectify inaccuracies, the right to be forgotten, and the right to object to processing.

3. **Canada**: The Personal Information Protection and Electronic Documents Act (PIPEDA) is Canada's primary law governing data privacy. PIPEDA applies to private-sector organisations that collect, use, or disclose personal information during commercial activities. PIPEDA requires organisations to obtain individuals' consent before collecting, using, or disclosing their personal information.

4. **Australia:** The Privacy Act is Australia's primary law governing data privacy. The Privacy Act applies to most Australian government agencies and private-sector organisations. It requires organisations to obtain an individual's consent before collecting, using, or disclosing their personal information and to take reasonable steps to protect that information.

5. **India:** The Digital Personal Data Protection Bill of 2023 introduces key regulations for managing digital personal data in India.

Here are its main features:

1. **Scope and Applicability**: The Bill governs the processing of digital personal data collected online and offline (but digitised) within India. It also extends to processing activities outside India, mainly when offering goods or services within the country.

2. **Consent and Lawful Processing**: Personal data can only be processed lawfully and requires the individual's consent, except for certain circumstances. These exceptions include voluntary data sharing by the individual or processing by the State for official purposes such as

issuing licenses, permits, or providing services and benefits.

3. **Obligations of Data Fiduciaries**: Entities handling personal data, termed 'data fiduciaries', must ensure data accuracy, safeguard data privacy and security, and delete data once its processing purpose is fulfilled.
4. **Individual Rights**: The Bill empowers individuals with specific rights. These include the right to access their data, request corrections, seek erasure of data, and address grievances.
5. **Government Exemptions**: The central government holds the authority to exempt certain government agencies from the Bill's provisions for national security, public order, and crime prevention.
6. **Regulatory Authority**: The Bill proposes the creation of the Data Protection Board of India. This body will oversee compliance and address the Bill's violations.

This Bill signifies a crucial step in regulating and protecting personal digital data in India, balancing individual rights with lawful data processing needs.

Carrying out a privacy assessment is an essential step for organisations to ensure they are complying with relevant privacy laws and regulations, protecting the privacy of their customers and users, and mitigating potential privacy risks. Here are the general steps to carry out a privacy assessment:

Identify the scope: Identify the scope of the privacy assessment, including the data types, systems, and processes that will be evaluated.

Conduct a data inventory: Conduct a data inventory to identify all data types and sources within the scope of the assessment. This can include personal data, sensitive data, and third-party data.

Assess privacy risks: Assess the privacy risks associated with the data types and sources identified in the data inventory. This can include assessing the likelihood and impact of potential privacy breaches or violations.

Review policies and procedures: Review the organisation's privacy policies and procedures to ensure they comply with relevant privacy laws and regulations and are aligned with industry best practices.

Assess third-party risks: Assess the privacy risks associated with third-party vendors or partners with access to the organisation's data. This can include reviewing contracts and agreements to ensure they include appropriate privacy and security requirements.

Develop a privacy risk mitigation plan: Develop a privacy risk mitigation plan that outlines specific measures to address identified privacy risks. This can include implementing new privacy controls, updating existing policies and procedures, and providing employee training.

Monitor and update: Monitor and update the privacy risk mitigation plan regularly to ensure ongoing compliance with privacy laws and regulations and address any new privacy risks.

Several free, open-source tools can assist with carrying out privacy assessments, including:

Open Privacy: An open-source framework for designing and implementing privacy-preserving systems.

OWASP Top 10 Privacy Risks: A list of the top 10 privacy risks in web applications and guidance on mitigating them.

Data Privacy Management Toolkit: A toolkit that guides the implementation of a privacy management program, including a privacy risk assessment.

PIA software: A privacy impact assessment software that can help organisations assess the impact of privacy risks associated with their data processing activities.

In summary, carrying out a privacy assessment is essential for organisations to ensure they are complying with relevant privacy laws and regulations, protecting the privacy of their customers and users, and mitigating potential privacy risks. Free, open-source tools are available to assist organisations with carrying out privacy assessments, including Open Privacy, OWASP Top 10 Privacy Risks, Data Privacy Management Toolkit, and PIA software.

Here's a list of open-source tools useful for discovering Personally Identifiable Information (PII):

1. **Data Sploit**: This tool excels in passive surveillance and intelligence gathering. It's adept at searching for PII across multiple platforms, including social media, email addresses, and domain names.
2. **Open PIV**: Open PIV specialises in identifying and extracting PII from structured and unstructured data sources. It can scan files like PDFs, images, and spreadsheets to pinpoint PII.
3. **DLP Toolkit**: As a data loss prevention tool, the DLP Toolkit uses machine learning to identify and classify sensitive data, including PII. It's customizable to align with specific organisational needs.
4. **OSSEC**: Operating as a host-based intrusion detection system, OSSEC can detect PII such as credit card and social security numbers. It offers real-time alerts on potential security incidents.
5. **Sensitive Data Finder**: This tool aids in identifying and classifying sensitive and PII data within an organisation's systems and databases. It's customizable and can integrate with other security tools for enhanced protection.

Each tool offers unique PII detection and protection capabilities, making them valuable assets for organisations looking to safeguard sensitive information.

The landscape of cyber threats is ever-evolving, making the continuous improvement and adaptation of Governance, Risk, and Compliance (GRC) strategies beneficial and essential for any organisation. This ongoing process of evaluation and adaptation is crucial in maintaining an effective defence against new and emerging risks.

Continuous Improvement: The key to staying ahead in cybersecurity is to embrace a continuous improvement mindset. This means regularly revisiting and refining GRC strategies to ensure they remain practical and relevant. It involves staying updated with the latest technological advancements and threat intelligence and incorporating this knowledge into your GRC framework. For instance, as new types of cyberattacks are identified, an organisation should assess whether its current security controls are adequate and make necessary adjustments.

Adaptation to Evolving Threats: Cyber threats are not static; they evolve rapidly as attackers devise new methods to exploit vulnerabilities. Organisations must, therefore, be agile in their response to these changes. This agility can be achieved through regular risk assessments, which help identify potential new vulnerabilities and threats. Based on these assessments, GRC strategies can be adapted to address specific risks more effectively.

Employee Training and Awareness: As part of continuous improvement, regular employee training and awareness programs are vital. Since human error can often be a weak link in security, keeping the workforce informed about the latest cyber threats and best practices is essential.

Technology and Tools Upgrade: Leveraging advanced tools and technologies play a significant role in adapting to new threats. This might include adopting more sophisticated cybersecurity software, utilising data analytics for better risk assessment, or employing artificial intelligence for enhanced threat detection and response.

Compliance with Changing Regulations: Compliance requirements are also subject to change as governments and regulatory bodies update laws to respond to new cyber realities. Continuous improvement in GRC involves staying abreast of these changes and ensuring that your organisation's practices comply with the latest regulatory standards.

In summary, the need for ongoing evaluation and adaptation of GRC strategies is pivotal in the current cybersecurity landscape. By embedding these practices into the organisational culture, businesses can not only protect themselves against present threats but also prepare for future challenges in the digital world.

Conclusion

As we conclude this chapter, let's revisit Sam's journey, a narrative encapsulating the quintessential challenges and triumphs of implementing ISO certification in a FinTech startup. Sam, who initially found himself in a maze of ISO standards and compliance complexities, stands today as a testament to the power of perseverance, structured planning, and adaptive learning.

Sam absorbed the essentials of ISO 27001 through the chapters, a standard that once seemed daunting. He learned the importance of establishing a robust information security management system (ISMS) and the nuances of risk assessment and management. Armed with this knowledge, Sam embarked on a systematic implementation plan. He assembled a cross-functional team, ensuring that every department contributed to and understood the significance of the ISO framework.

Sam's journey wasn't without its hurdles. He navigated through resource constraints, tight deadlines, and the challenge of aligning his startup's dynamic operations with the stringent requirements of ISO 27001. However, what made his journey successful was his commitment to continuous learning and improvement. Sam ensured that his team followed procedures and understood the 'why' behind each action. He fostered an organisational culture that embraced security as a core value, not just a compliance requirement.

His meticulous planning paid off during the audit phase. The auditor's scrutiny revealed a well-structured ISMS deeply integrated into the startup's operations. Sam's team demonstrated compliance with ISO standards and a genuine commitment to information security.

Today, as Sam looks back, he sees more than just an ISO certification; he sees a transformation in his startup's approach to information security. This journey has elevated the startup's credibility in the eyes of clients and partners and has laid a strong foundation for sustainable growth and resilience in the face of evolving cyber threats.

Sam's story is a beacon for any professional embarking on the ISO certification path. It highlights that with the right approach, unwavering dedication, and a willingness to learn and adapt, achieving ISO certification is an attainable goal and a catalyst for broader organisational excellence.

Chapter - 3

Overview: FOrtifying YOur Digital FOrtress - ApplicatiOn Security and The Secure SOftware DevelOpment Lifecycle (SDLC)

Can we write a better intro paragraph?

Imagine this: your startup has just launched its flagship app. Users are signing up, investors are watching, and growth is skyrocketing. Then, within weeks, a security flaw in the code is exploited. Customer data is leaked, trust evaporates, and the brand you worked so hard to build is suddenly in crisis.

This isn't a rare story; it's the reality many young companies face. The root cause? Security treated as an afterthought. Application Security and the Secure Software Development Lifecycle (SDLC) aim to flip this narrative. By embedding security into every phase of development- from design to deployment — you can stop vulnerabilities before they surface and build products that inspire trust rather than fear.

In this chapter, we'll explore how Secure SDLC transforms software development into not just a creative process, but a protective one; fortifying your digital fortress before attackers ever test its walls.

Application Security

Web application security is a pressing and widely discussed topic in today's digital landscape. The stakes are high for businesses relying on internet commerce, users entrusting sensitive information to web applications, and criminals seeking to exploit vulnerabilities for financial gain. A critical factor is reputation, as insecure websites lose trust and jeopardise customer relationships. However, acquiring reliable information about the current state of web application security is challenging due to organisations' reluctance to disclose vulnerabilities or breaches.

Application architecture has changed dramatically over the last five-to- ten years. Applications have evolved from running on a single server to an abstract collection of virtual machines (VMs) and services (such as SaaS, microservices, and containers) that deliver the application. To further complicate matters, those services and VMs may not all run from the same location. Traditional approaches mostly require policy to be written in terms of the network (e.g., an IP address), and in today's dynamic datacenter, this requirement makes policy management a frequent and painful process.

Application security risks are a major concern in the technology industry. With the increasing reliance on web and mobile applications, the potential for security breaches and data loss is higher than ever before.

The chapter addresses a fundamental security challenge faced by web applications: the acceptance of arbitrary user input. It examines the factors that weaken their security posture and offers insights into emerging trends in web application security. Understanding these trends is essential for startups and security professionals aiming to stay ahead of evolving threats and adopt proactive security measures. By addressing these vulnerabilities and staying informed on security developments, your startup can build a more secure and resilient foundation.

Integrating Security into the Software Development Lifecycle (SDLC)

The fundamentals of securing the Software Development Lifecycle (SDLC) revolve around the integration of security practices into each stage of software development, creating a holistic and proactive approach to cybersecurity. It begins with the planning phase, where security requirements are identified and incorporated into the project objectives. In the design phase, these requirements translate into secure architecture and design choices. During development, coding practices include regular code reviews and vulnerability assessments to ensure security measures are correctly implemented. Testing is another critical stage, involving rigorous security testing alongside functional testing to uncover and fix security flaws. As the software moves to deployment, security configurations and access controls are meticulously checked and enforced.

Post-deployment, continuous monitoring and regular updates are crucial for maintaining software security against emerging threats. This lifecycle approach ensures that security is not an add-on but an integral part of the software development process, leading to more secure and robust software products.

Alarming Vulnerabilities in Web Applications: A Comprehensive Analysis

Through extensive testing of numerous web applications, we have discovered alarming vulnerabilities. Broken authentication, affecting 62% of tested applications, exposes flaws in login mechanisms that allow attackers to guess weak passwords or bypass authentication altogether. Broken access controls, found in 71% of applications, inadequately protect sensitive data and functionalities, enabling unauthorised access.

SQL injection, present in 32% of tested applications, allows attackers to manipulate input and interfere with back-end databases, potentially retrieving sensitive data or executing commands. Cross-site scripting, discovered in a staggering 94% of applications, empowers attackers to target other users, gain unauthorised access to their data, and carry out various attacks.

Information leakage, observed in 78% of applications, occurs when sensitive information is inadvertently disclosed, aiding attackers in planning assaults. Additionally, cross-site request forgery, affecting 92% of applications, manipulates users into performing unintended actions within the application, granting malicious websites interaction privileges.

In the realm of application security, various cyberattacks pose threats to web applications. Here's a rundown of some common types:

- **SQL Injection:** Attackers exploit vulnerabilities in input validation to inject malicious SQL code into an application's database. This can compromise data integrity and confidentiality.
- **Cross-Site Scripting (XSS):** This involves embedding malicious scripts into web pages viewed by others. It can lead to unauthorised actions like cookie theft, session hijacking, or redirecting users to harmful sites.

- **Cross-Site Request Forgery (CSRF):** Here, users are deceived into performing actions they didn't intend on a website, like changing email addresses or passwords, often without realising it.
- **File Inclusion Vulnerabilities:** These allow attackers to include harmful files from external sources into web pages, potentially leading to arbitrary code execution.
- **Distributed Denial-of-Service (DDoS) Attacks:** These attacks aim to flood a web server with excessive traffic, rendering the website inaccessible to legitimate users.
- **Phishing and Spear-Phishing:** These deceptive attacks trick users into divulging sensitive information, such as login details, by masquerading as trustworthy entities.
- **Password Attacks:** This category includes methods like brute force or guessing to crack passwords and gain unauthorised access to web applications.
- **Application Logic Attacks:** Attackers manipulate the application's logic by altering input data or requests, which can result in unauthorised access, data theft, or escalated privileges.

Key Problem Factors

By comprehending the current state of application security and its challenges, readers can better appreciate the need for diligent security practices. The chapter sets the stage for subsequent discussions on effective security strategies, best practices, and the implementation of comprehensive security measures to safeguard web applications from potential threats and vulnerabilities.

Architecting application security involves designing and implementing security measures throughout the application development process to protect against potential vulnerabilities and threats.

Here are some steps to architect application security:

1. **Start with a secure design**: Implement security from the beginning of the development process by creating a secure design that considers potential threats and vulnerabilities. This includes using secure coding

practices, following industry standards and guidelines, and using secure design patterns.

2. **Identify and protect sensitive data:** Identify and classify sensitive data and implement appropriate controls to protect it. This may include encryption, access controls, and monitoring.
3. **Implement authentication and access controls:** Use a robust authentication and access control mechanism to ensure that only authorised users can access the application and its resources. This can include implementing multi-factor authentication, role-based access controls, and least privilege principles.
4. **Use a defence-in-depth approach:** Implement multiple layers of security to protect against a wide range of threats. This can include firewalls, intrusion detection/prevention systems, and security information and event management (SIEM) systems.
5. **Regularly test and monitor**: Regularly test and monitor the application for vulnerabilities and potential threats. This includes using automated tools to scan for vulnerabilities, penetration testing, and monitoring for suspicious activity.
6. **Continuously improve**: Continuously improve the application security by staying informed about the latest threats and vulnerabilities and implementing new security measures as needed.
7. **Train your team:** Make sure that your team is trained in security best practices and that they understand the importance of security in the development process.

There is a common belief among users that web applications are secure due to the use of SSL technology and compliance with standards.

Frequently, application FAQs reassure users that their personal information is protected and that regular scans are conducted to ensure security. However, despite these claims, the reality is that most web applications remain insecure.

Before we start this paragraph, we need to add some context or a head start.

There are several key areas of focus in application security, including:

- **Input validation:** This involves ensuring that any data entered into an application, such as through a web form, is properly sanitised and validated. This can help prevent attacks such as SQL injection, where an attacker injects malicious code into a form field to gain access to sensitive data.
- **Authentication and access control**: This involves ensuring that only authorised users can access specific parts of an application, and that they are properly authenticated. This can include implementing multi-factor authentication, as well as using role-based access control to ensure that users only have access to the parts of the application that they need.
- **Security testing:** This involves testing an application for vulnerabilities, such as by using automated tools or manual penetration testing. This can help identify and fix potential security issues before they can be exploited by attackers.
- **Secure coding practices**: This involves developing applications using secure coding practices, such as following OWASP guidelines, to help prevent common vulnerabilities such as buffer overflows, cross-site scripting (XSS), and cross-site request forgery (CSRF).
- **Monitoring and incident response**: This involves monitoring for signs of an attack, such as unusual traffic patterns, and having a plan in place for responding to a security incident. This can include incident response teams, incident response plans, and incident management software.
- **Conducting regular security assessments**: This involves regularly testing applications for vulnerabilities, both internally and externally, and taking steps to address any issues that are identified.
- **Implementing a secure software development lifecycle (SSDL):** This involves following a structured process for developing, testing, and deploying secure applications, including security requirements gathering, secure design, secure coding, and

security testing.

- **Conducting regular security training**: This involves providing regular security training to developers, including training on secure coding practices, and providing them with the tools and resources they need to develop secure applications.
- **Keeping software up to date:** This involves regularly applying security updates and patches to all applications and software, including third-party software and libraries.
- **Implementing a security incident response plan**: This involves having a plan in place for responding to security incidents, including incident response teams, incident response plans, and incident management software.

For startups, the main security issue in applications is dealing with untrusted, potentially harmful data. This problem is made worse by several factors in web applications, leading to common poor security practices.

Underdeveloped Security Awareness:

Web application security is a relatively newer field compared to network and operating system security. While awareness has grown, many IT security professionals still lack a comprehensive understanding of core concepts in web application security. Developers often rely on third-party packages without fully understanding their security implications, leading to assumptions and misconceptions about the security provided.

Let's look at some of the reasons why application security needs to be integrated all the way -

Custom Development:

Most web applications are developed in-house or by third-party contractors, resulting in customised code and unique defects in each application. Unlike infrastructure deployments, where industry-standard guidelines can be followed, web applications vary widely in their security posture due to custom development practices.

Deceptive Simplicity:

Modern web application platforms and development tools make it easy for novice programmers to create functional applications quickly. However, the simplicity of development does not guarantee security. Well-intentioned individuals without extensive security knowledge may overlook potential vulnerabilities during the development process.

Figure 1.3 The incidence of some common web application vulnerabilities in applications recently tested by the authors (based on a sample of more than 100)

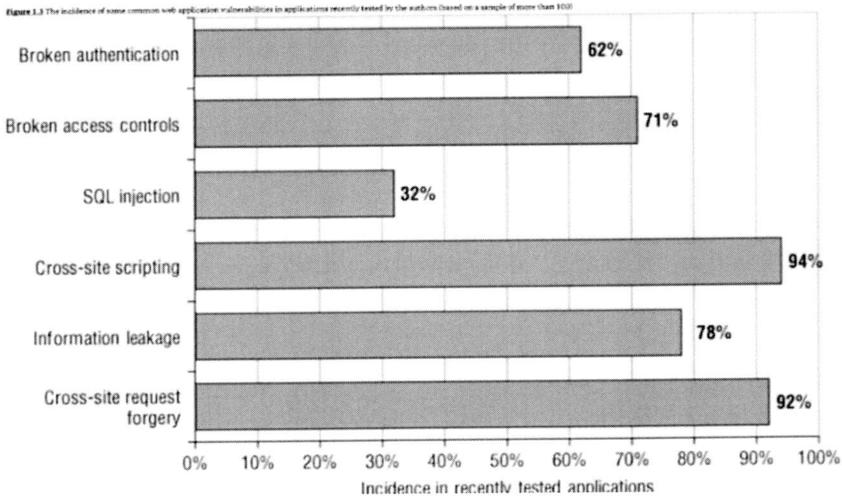

Application Frameworks:

Application frameworks have gained popularity as they offer pre-built code components for common functionality. While these frameworks streamline development, they also lead to a widespread use of similar components across different applications. Consequently, a vulnerability discovered in one framework can impact numerous unrelated applications, amplifying the potential risks.

Rapidly Evolving Threat Profile:

Web application attacks and defenses evolve at a rapid pace. New attack techniques are continually discovered, rendering previously accepted defenses ineffective. Development teams may start a project with current threat knowledge but find it outdated by the time the application is deployed, requiring ongoing vigilance and adaptation.

Resource and Time Constraints:

Web application development projects often face constraints in terms of time and resources. Organizations may lack dedicated security expertise within development teams and rely on specialists for security testing, which is often deferred until late in the project's life cycle due to time limitations. This can result in insufficient security measures being implemented.

Understanding these key problem factors is crucial for addressing the challenges of web application security effectively. By recognising the underlying issues and their impact, organisations can prioritise security measures, invest in security training, and implement robust security practices throughout the development life cycle.

These statistics above demonstrate that despite claims of security, applications are far from immune to vulnerabilities. It is essential to recognise the need for comprehensive security measures and continuous testing to identify and address these weaknesses. By understanding the prevalent vulnerabilities, readers can better comprehend the criticality of robust security practices and take appropriate steps to protect their web applications.

While building applications, developers often rely on the Software Development Life Cycle (SDLC) as their guiding framework. A Secure SDLC takes this model a step further by embedding security practices into every stage of development. Each phase- from planning to maintenance, carries unique responsibilities that collectively shape the security posture of the final product. By understanding and applying these phases with security in mind, startups can move beyond simply delivering functional software to creating systems that are resilient, trustworthy, and built to withstand evolving threats.

Let's delve into each phase and understand its significance in achieving robust security.

1. **Requirements Gathering**: At the outset, the project team identifies and documents the software's functional and security requirements. These requirements serve as the bedrock for the entire development process. Thoroughly gathering and documenting security requirements is crucial to grasping the software's security goals, threat landscape, and compliance obligations.

2. **Design**: In the design phase, security considerations are woven into the overall system architecture and detailed design. Robust and resilient software systems are built by applying secure design principles and best practices. Security controls like access controls,

encryption mechanisms, and error handling are identified and integrated into the system's design to tackle potential vulnerabilities and mitigate threats.

3. **Coding**: In the coding phase, developers translate the design specifications into actual software code. They follow secure coding practices, including input validation, output encoding, and proper error handling. By adhering to secure coding guidelines, developers establish a strong foundation for a more secure software system, thwarting common vulnerabilities like injection attacks, cross-site scripting, and buffer overflows.
4. **Testing**: The testing phase concentrates on identifying and eliminating security vulnerabilities and weaknesses within the software. It encompasses various testing types, such as functional testing, security testing, and penetration testing. Techniques like vulnerability scanning and code review are employed for security testing, uncovering vulnerabilities that malicious actors could exploit. Comprehensive testing ensures that the software adheres to the specified security requirements and operates securely under diverse scenarios.
5. **Deployment:** Once the software has undergone thorough testing and is deemed secure, it is ready for deployment. During this phase, security controls, configurations, and policies are implemented to fortify the software within its operational environment. Measures may include securing servers, hardening configurations, implementing secure network protocols, and establishing appropriate user access controls. Secure deployment practices minimise the risk of unauthorised access and guarantee the software's secure operation in a production environment.
6. **Maintenance**: The maintenance phase involves ongoing support and updates for the software system. This encompasses addressing security vulnerabilities and applying patches as new threats emerge. Regular security audits, monitoring, and incident response processes are established to ensure the software's ongoing security. By actively maintaining and updating the software, organisations can proactively address security issues and uphold a secure environment throughout

the software's lifecycle.

Essential Security Practices for Startups: Tools and Strategies

Requirements Gathering:

Best Practices: Involve security stakeholders early, conduct threat modelling exercises, and implement security questionnaires or checklists.

Tools: Threat Modeller (commercial) helps with threat modelling, while OWASP Risk Rating Methodology (free) provides a framework for assessing risks.

Design:

Best Practices: Apply secure design principles, conduct security architecture reviews, and utilise threat modelling techniques.

Tools: Microsoft Threat Modelling Tool (free) aids in designing secure architectures, while OWASP Application Security Verification Standard (free) offers guidelines for secure design practices.

Coding:

Best Practices: Adhere to secure coding practices, follow coding guidelines, and conduct code reviews.

Tools: SonarQube (free and commercial) provides static code analysis to identify vulnerabilities, while Veracode (commercial) offers a comprehensive application security platform.

Testing:

Best Practices: Perform comprehensive security testing, including vulnerability scanning, penetration testing, and security code reviews.

Tools: OWASP ZAP (free) and Burp Suite (free and commercial) are widely used for web application security testing. Nessus (commercial) and OpenVAS (free) are popular vulnerability scanners.

Deployment:

Best Practices: Follow secure deployment practices, implement secure configurations, and conduct vulnerability assessments.

Tools: Chef (commercial) and Puppet (open-source) are configuration management tools that automate secure server configurations.

Maintenance:

Best Practices: Establish vulnerability management processes, implement patch management, and conduct regular security audits.

Tools: Qualys (commercial) and Nexpose (commercial) are vulnerability management solutions, while OpenVAS (free) can also be used for ongoing vulnerability scanning.

Building a strong Dev Sec Ops practice involves integrating security into the entire DevOps workflow, from development to deployment and operations. Here are some key steps and tools that can be used to achieve this:

Security Culture: Foster a security-focused mindset and culture across the organisation. Encourage collaboration between developers, operations teams, and security professionals to prioritise security throughout the development process.

Automation: Utilise automation tools to ensure consistent and repeatable security practices. This includes automating code analysis, vulnerability scanning, security testing, and deployment processes.

Tools: Jenkins, GitLab, and Circle CI are popular continuous integration/continuous deployment (CI/CD) tools that support automation. These tools can be extended with security plugins and integrations, such as SonarQube for code analysis, OWASP ZAP for security testing, and vulnerability scanners like Nessus or OpenVAS.

Infrastructure as Code (IaC):

Implement infrastructure as code practices to manage and provision infrastructure resources. This helps maintain consistency, enables version control, and allows for security configurations to be applied consistently across environments.

Tools: Infrastructure as code tools like Terraform and AWS CloudFormation can be used to define and deploy infrastructure resources. Configuration management tools like Chef, Puppet, or Ansible can automate the configuration of security settings.

Continuous Security Testing:

Embed security testing throughout the development pipeline to identify vulnerabilities early and minimise risks. This includes static code analysis, dynamic application security testing (DAST), and interactive application security testing (IAST).

Tools: SonarQube, Veracode, and Check are examples of static code analysis tools. OWASP ZAP and Burp Suite are widely used for dynamic application security testing.

Secure Code Development:

Promote secure coding practices within the development teams. Provide training and resources to educate developers on common security vulnerabilities and best practices for secure coding.

Tools: IDE plugins like SonarLint or ESLint with security rulesets can help developers identify and fix security issues as they write code. Secure coding guidelines, such as those provided by OWASP, can serve as references.

Continuous Monitoring and Incident Response:

Implement robust monitoring and incident response capabilities to detect and respond to security incidents promptly. Monitor systems, applications, and network traffic to identify and mitigate potential threats.

Tools: Security Information and Event Management (SIEM) tools like Splunk or ELK stack (Elasticsearch, Logstash, Kibana) can help aggregate and analyse security logs. Intrusion Detection and Prevention Systems (IDS/IPS) like Snort or Suricata can aid in monitoring network traffic for suspicious activities.

Collaboration and Communication:

Foster strong collaboration and communication between development, operations, and security teams. Encourage cross-functional teams and establish channels for sharing security-related information and best practices.

Tools: Collaboration tools like Slack, Microsoft Teams, or Atlassian Confluence can facilitate communication and knowledge sharing among team members.

Let's explore some of the key defence mechanisms that startups can use to secure their web applications:

1. **User Access Management:** This mechanism controls user access to the application's data and functionality, ensuring that unauthorised users are prevented from gaining entry. It involves authentication, authorisation, and user privilege management to enforce proper access controls.
2. **User Input Handling:** Web applications must properly handle user input to prevent malicious or malformed data from causing undesirable behaviour or opening avenues for exploitation. Robust input validation and sanitisation techniques are employed to mitigate risks associated with input-based vulnerabilities.
3. **Defence against Attackers:** Web applications need to withstand direct attacks. This involves implementing defensive measures, such as intrusion detection and prevention systems, firewalls, and security incident response mechanisms. Additionally, offensive measures, like honeypots or deception techniques, may be employed to frustrate attackers.
4. **Application Management:** Effective management of the application itself is crucial for ensuring its security. This includes monitoring activities, detecting and responding to security incidents, and configuring the application's functionality securely. Administrators play a vital role in maintaining the application's security posture.
5. **Endpoint Security:** Endpoint security refers to the practice of securing individual devices—known as endpoints—that connect to a network. These include laptops, desktops, smartphones, tablets, servers, and even IoT devices. Each endpoint serves as a potential entry point for cyber threats such as malware, ransomware, phishing attacks, and unauthorised access.

Unified Endpoint Management and Security Solutions from Managengine

In the startup world, where remote work, BYOD (Bring Your Own Device), and hybrid teams are the norm, endpoint security is not optional—it's mission-critical.

Whether it's a developer's laptop, a sales rep's tablet, or a test mobile device, each endpoint is a potential entry point for attackers. Centralised control over these endpoints is essential to protect your infrastructure and customer data.

ManageEngine's unified endpoint management and security (UEMS) solutions provide centralised control to effectively secure and manage all endpoints, help startups mitigate security vulnerabilities, ensure compliance, and scale securely without compromising operational agility.

Key Capabilities Include:

- **Automated patching:** Automated patch deployment for Windows, Mac, Linux, and third-party applications.
- **Threat detection and remediation:** Detect known and unknown threats with deep-learning ML and behavioral analytics.
- **Ransomware protection:** Gain insights into the root cause of ransomware attacks to provide immediate incident response and prevent future attacks.
- **Vulnerability management:** Monitor and identify both publicly disclosed vulnerabilities and zero-day threats, rank them based on their impact, urgency, and patch availability to ensure an up-to-date security posture.
- **Next-gen antivirus:** Provide proactive defence against sophisticated cyberthreats that traditional antivirus programs might miss by utilising AI, behaviour-based analysis, and deep learning algorithms.
- **BYOD security:** Separate corporate data by containerising it. Apply security policies to these containers, including restrictions on data sharing,

Key ManageEngine product: Endpoint Central

Visit www.manageengine.com/uems to know more.

These defence mechanisms not only address the core security problem but also form the majority of a web application's attack surface. Understanding these mechanisms thoroughly is essential for both defensive and offensive security practices. Whether you are new to web application hacking or experienced in the field, taking the time to comprehend how these core mechanisms function in each application encountered is vital. By identifying their weak points, vulnerabilities can be exploited effectively, enabling better security testing and mitigation strategies.

Let's delve into additional strategies for bolstering the security defences of applications:

Managing user access is a key pillar of application security, essential for almost every app out there. It's all about who gets to see and do what within your application. Think of it as giving out keys to different rooms in a building. You have various user levels – like visitors (anonymous users), regular users (authenticated users), and bosses (administrators). Each group should only access certain areas. For example, in a web mail app, users should only read their own emails and not anyone else's.

To handle this, web apps usually use a trio of security measures:

1. **Authentication:** This is your front door. It's about making sure a user is who they say they are. Without it, you can't tell friend from foe. Most apps use a username and password, but for extra security, some add more steps – like codes from a smartphone or fingerprint scans.

2. **Session Management:** Once a user is in, you need to keep track of them – that's session management. It's like giving them a visitor badge that expires. You assign a unique ID to each session and make sure it ends when the user logs out or after a certain time.

3. **Access Control:** This is about setting up barriers – deciding who gets access to what. It's like having locked doors inside your building. You might use role-based access (where different roles have set permissions) or more flexible rules based on user attributes.

Each of these mechanisms is crucial, and they need to work together seamlessly. If one fails, it can leave a gap for attackers to slip through. So, it's important to carefully plan and regularly check these security measures to ensure they're up to the task.

Remember Sam, a diligent software security engineer at a FinTech startup? He was tasked with enhancing the security of their Application Programming Interface (API), a crucial component that allowed their application to communicate and exchange data seamlessly. Aware of the rising cyber threats, Sam embarked on a mission to fortify their APIs. Here's how he did it:

1. **Authentication and Authorisation:** Sam started by integrating robust authentication methods like OAuth 2.0 and JSON Web Tokens (JWT) to verify the identity of users accessing the API. He also implemented strict authorisation checks to ensure users could only access data they were permitted to, much like having different levels of security clearance.
2. **Input Validation and Sanitisation:** He made sure every piece of data passing through the API was checked and cleaned. This was like having a security checkpoint to ensure no malicious code or data slipped through.
3. **HTTPS Implementation:** Sam ensured all API communications were done over HTTPS, encrypting data in transit. It was akin to sending confidential messages in a secure, sealed envelope.
4. **API Gateways:** He set up an API gateway, acting as a sentinel to oversee and manage API traffic. The gateway provided extra layers of security, like rate limiting and access control, much like a border checkpoint manages who comes in and out of a country.
5. **API Keys:** Sam employed API keys for additional security. These keys were like special passes for applications to make API calls, kept secret and regularly changed to prevent unauthorised access.
6. **Logging and Monitoring:** He implemented logging of all API activities and set up monitoring for unusual patterns or signs of a breach, similar to having surveillance cameras and security guards keeping watch.

7. **Regular Security Testing:** Sam conducted routine security drills, testing the API for vulnerabilities and addressing any weaknesses found, much like a building inspector checking for structural integrity.

8. **Server-Side Validation:** Finally, he ensured that validations were also done server-side, providing a backstop in case client-side checks were bypassed.

Through these steps, Sam elevated the security of his organization's APIs. He understood that securing APIs was not a one-time task, but an ongoing process, requiring constant vigilance and adaptation to new threats. With his efforts, Sam not only protected the company's data and systems but also gained the trust of their clients and users.

In his quest to fortify the application's security, Sam realised the importance of conducting a thorough secure source code review. Here's how he approached it:

1. **Define the Scope:** Sam began by clearly outlining the scope of the review. He identified which parts of the codebase needed examination and pinpointed specific security aspects to focus on, such as sensitive data handling and authentication processes.

2. **Identify the Team:** He put together a diverse team consisting of developers, security experts, and other relevant stakeholders. This team was responsible for the comprehensive review of the code, bringing together different perspectives and expertise.

3. **Establish a Checklist:** Sam created a checklist based on security best practices and guidelines, drawing from resources like the OWASP Top 10, SANS Top 25, and CERT Secure Coding Standards. This checklist served as a roadmap for the review process.

4. **Use of Automated Tools:** He utilised automated tools for an initial scan of the codebase, identifying known vulnerabilities. These tools provided a preliminary report of potential issues that needed further inspection.

5. **Manual Code Review:** The team also conducted a manual, line-by-line review of the code. They were particularly vigilant for issues that automated tools might miss, such as hard-coded credentials or weak encryption methods.

6. **Prioritise and Track Issues:** After identifying various issues, Sam prioritized them based on their potential impact and tracked their resolution process, ensuring no vulnerability was left unaddressed.

7. **Provide Feedback:** He made sure to provide detailed feedback to the development team. This feedback included not only the identified issues but also recommendations for improvements and best practices.

8. **Follow-up Review:** Finally, Sam established a process for follow-up reviews. These were crucial to ensure that all identified issues were properly resolved and to maintain the security integrity of the codebase over time.

By integrating this secure code review process into the software development lifecycle (SDLC), Sam helped his team catch and rectify security vulnerabilities early on. This proactive approach not only enhanced the security of their product but also saved the company significant time and resources, which might otherwise have been spent addressing issues post-deployment. Under Sam's guidance, the team developed a deeper understanding of secure coding practices, making security a fundamental aspect of their development process.

Top 10 Web Application Security Risks

There are three new categories, four categories with naming and scoping changes, and some consolidation in the Top 10 for 2021.

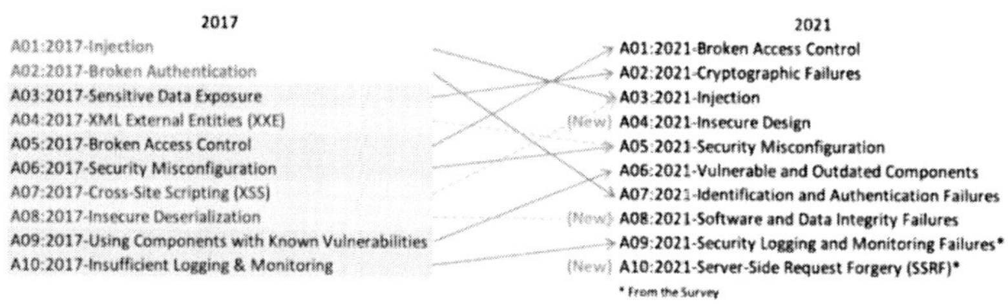

1. A01:2021-Broken Access Control moves up from the fifth position; 94% of applications were tested for some form of broken access control. The 34 Common Weakness Enumerations (CWEs) mapped to Broken Access Control had more occurrences in applications than any other category.

2. A02:2021-Cryptographic Failures shifts up one position to #2, previously known as Sensitive Data Exposure, which was broad symptom rather than a root cause. The renewed focus here is on failures related to cryptography which often leads to sensitive data

exposure or system compromise.

3. A03:2021-Injection slides down to the third position. 94% of the applications were tested for some form of injection, and the 33 CWEs mapped into this category have the second most occurrences in applications. Cross-site Scripting is now part of this category in this edition.

4. A04:2021-Insecure Design is a new category for 2021, with a focus on risks related to design flaws. If we genuinely want to "move left" as an industry, it calls for more use of threat modeling, secure design patterns and principles, and reference architectures.

5. A05:2021-Security Misconfiguration moves up from #6 in the previous edition; 90% of applications were tested for some form of misconfiguration. With more shifts into highly configurable software, it's not surprising to see this category move up. The former category for XML External Entities (XXE) is now part of this category.

6. A06:2021-Vulnerable and Outdated Components was previously titled Using Components with Known Vulnerabilities and is #2 in the Top 10 community survey, but also had enough data to make the Top 10 via data analysis. This category moves up from #9 in 2017 and is a known issue that we struggle to test and assess risk. It is the only category not to have any Common Vulnerability and Exposures (CVEs) mapped to the included CWEs, so a default exploit and impact weights of 5.0 are factored into their scores.

7. A07:2021-Identification and Authentication Failures was previously Broken Authentication and is sliding down from the second position, and now includes CWEs that are more related to identification failures. This category is still an integral part of the Top 10, but the increased availability of standardised frameworks seems to be helping.

8. A08:2021-Software and Data Integrity Failures is a new category for 2021, focusing on making assumptions related to software updates, critical data, and CI/CD pipelines without verifying integrity. One of the highest weighted impacts from Common Vulnerability and Exposures/Common Vulnerability Scoring System (CVE/CVSS) data mapped to the 10 CWEs in this category. Insecure Deserialization from 2017 is now a part of this larger category.

9. A09:2021-Security Logging and Monitoring Failures was previously Insufficient Logging & Monitoring and is added from the industry survey (#3), moving up from #10 previously. This category is expanded to include more types of failures, is challenging to test for, and isn't well represented in the CVE/CVSS data. However, failures in this category can directly impact visibility, incident alerting, and forensics.

10. A10:2021-Server-Side Request Forgery is added from the Top 10 community survey (#1). The data shows a relatively low incidence rate with above average testing coverage, along with above-average ratings for Exploit and Impact potential. This category represents the scenario where the security community members are telling us this is important, even though it's not illustrated in the data at this time.

This requires more story telling like how he did it - instead of only line by line

Sam, now tasked with ensuring the security of his company's web application, approached the challenge methodically. Here's how he went about it:

1. **Configure Proxy/Spidering Tool:** Sam set up his browser to work with a tool like Burp Suite or Web Scarab. This allowed him to passively monitor web content and spider the site.

2. **Browser Extensions for Monitoring**: He used extensions like IEWatch to keep a close eye on HTTP and HTML content processed by the browser.

3. **Thorough Browsing:** Sam meticulously browsed the entire application, exploring every link, URL, and form. He tested different browser settings to see how they affected the application's behavior.

4. **Authenticated Access Testing**: For areas requiring login, Sam used his account to check for secure access to protected functionalities.

5. **Monitoring Requests and Responses:** Using his proxy tool, Sam examined the data flow between the client and server, gaining insights into how user input affected the application.

6. **Reviewing Spidered Content**: He checked the site map generated by the passive spidering tool to identify any unexplored areas and then

manually visited them.

7. **Active Crawling**: Post manual exploration, Sam employed active spidering to find additional content that might have been missed earlier.

8. **Consulting Public Resources:** He used search engines and resources like the Wayback Machine to find indexed or archived content related to the application.

9. **Discovering Hidden Content:** Sam experimented with different requests to understand how the application responded to nonexistent items, helping him identify hidden content.

10. **Testing Default Content with Nikto:** He ran tools like Nikto against the web server to identify any default or well-known content.

11. **Understanding Authentication Mechanisms**: Sam determined what authentication technologies were used and located all related functionalities in the application.

12. **Testing Password Quality**: He checked the application's rules for password strength and tried setting weak passwords to test its resilience.

13. **Checking for Username Enumeration**: Sam carefully tested various parts of the application where usernames were submitted, looking for ways an attacker might enumerate usernames.

14. **Assessing Resilience to Password Guessing:** He tested the application's response to multiple invalid login attempts to check for account lockout mechanisms.

15. **Evaluating Account Recovery Functions:** Sam also examined the application's process for account recovery, looking for security weaknesses.

Securing a Web3 application, with its unique challenges and decentralised nature, required Sam to adapt and refine his approach. Here's how he tackled the task, point by point:

1. **Understand the Web3 Environment**: Sam began by deepening his understanding of blockchain and decentralised technologies, essential for Web3 applications.

2. **Smart Contract Security:** He focused on securing smart contracts, which are pivotal in Web3. This involved conducting thorough audits, both automated and manual, to check for vulnerabilities like reentrancy, overflow/underflow, and gas limit issues.

3. **Private Key Management**: Sam implemented robust mechanisms for private key management, ensuring they were securely stored and not exposed to potential breaches.

4. **Decentralised Identity Verification:** He incorporated decentralised identity verification methods to enhance user authentication without compromising privacy.

5. **Front-End Security**: Despite the decentralised nature of Web3, Sam recognised the importance of securing the front-end. He ensured that the client-side code was resilient against common web vulnerabilities like XSS and CSRF.

6. **Blockchain Node Security:** He set up secure, reliable node connections for the application, minimising the risk of exposing the app to compromised nodes.

7. **Data Privacy and Encryption:** Sam ensured that data on the blockchain was appropriately encrypted and that privacy standards were maintained, considering the immutable nature of blockchain data.

8. **Decentralised Application (Dapp) Security Audits**: Regular security audits for the Dapp were conducted to identify and fix any security gaps.

9. **Monitoring and Incident Response:** He established a system for continuous monitoring of the application's activity, ready to respond quickly to any security incidents.

10. **Staying Updated with Web3 Security Trends**: Finally, Sam committed to staying informed about the latest security trends and threats in the Web3 space, adapting his strategies accordingly.

Through these steps, Sam successfully navigated the complex landscape of Web3 security, ensuring that the application was not only functional and user-friendly but also secure and trustworthy.

By taking these steps, Sam methodically tested the application's security, ensuring that it was fortified against a variety of potential attacks. His approach highlighted the importance of a comprehensive and systematic security testing strategy in application development.

Start with a paragraph before starting to talk about securing Node.js

Securing Node.js in application development is critical for several compelling reasons:

- **Popularity Attracts Vulnerabilities**: Node.js, being one of the most popular JavaScript runtimes, is a common target for attackers. Its popularity means a larger potential impact for any vulnerability exploited, making it a lucrative target.
- **Sensitive Data Handling**: Node.js is often used in applications that handle sensitive data, including personal user information and financial transactions. Securing Node.js applications is essential to protect this data from unauthorised access and breaches, which could lead to significant financial and reputational damage.
- **NPM Ecosystem Risks**: The vast npm ecosystem, while a strength, also poses security risks. Dependencies on third-party modules can introduce vulnerabilities. Ensuring security in Node.js means carefully managing these modules, including regular updates and audits.
- **Real-Time Applications**: Node.js is commonly used for real-time applications like chat applications, online gaming, and collaborative tools. These applications require robust security to prevent real-time data breaches and to maintain user trust and integrity.
- **Preventing Injection Attacks**: Node.js applications can be susceptible to injection attacks like SQL Injection (SQLi) and Cross-Site Scripting (XSS) if not properly secured. These attacks can lead to data loss, corruption, and unauthorized access.
- **Scalability and Performance**: As Node.js applications scale, the surface area for potential attacks increases. Proper security measures are crucial to ensure that, as the application grows, it remains resilient to attacks without compromising on performance.

Node.js

Node.js is a popular JavaScript runtime environment that is widely used for building web and mobile applications. Here are several steps organisations can take to secure their Node.js applications:

1. **Keep Node.js and its dependencies up to date**: This involves regularly updating Node.js and its dependencies to ensure that the application is protected from known vulnerabilities.
2. **Input validation and sanitisation:** This involves validating and sanitising all input data received by the application to ensure that it is in the correct format and does not contain any malicious code or data.
3. **Use of secure session management:** This involves using secure session management techniques, such as using secure cookies or JSON Web Tokens (JWT), to ensure that sessions are properly authenticated and protected from session hijacking.
4. **Use of encryption:** This involves using encryption to protect sensitive data, such as user credentials and financial transactions.
5. **Use of access control**: This involves implementing access control mechanisms to ensure that only authorised users can access specific parts of the application.
6. **Use of logging and monitoring**: This involves logging all API calls and monitoring for any suspicious activity. This can help identify and address security incidents.
7. **Use of a web application firewall (WAF)**: This involves using a WAF to protect the application from web-based attacks, such as SQL injection and cross-site scripting (XSS).
8. **Use of security modules and libraries:** This involves using security modules and libraries, such as Helmet and cores, to provide additional security features to the application.

It's important to remember that Node.js is just like any other technology, and it's only as secure as the code that runs on it. Therefore, it's important to follow secure coding practices, such as OWASP guidelines, and regularly review the code to ensure it is secure. Additionally, it's important to stay informed about the latest security threats and vulnerabilities specific to Node.js and its dependencies and update them accordingly.

Application Threat Modelling

Let's dwell upon our story of Sam, who was recently tasked with developing and securing a cutting-edge financial product that promised to revolutionise the way people manage their finances. Eager to make his mark, Sam dived headfirst into the development process, coding away with zeal and precision.

As Sam was knee-deep in lines of code, his team decided to bring in a cybersecurity consultant, Ms. Rivera, to ensure their product was as secure as it was innovative. During one of their development meetings, Ms. Rivera introduced the concept of "Application Threat Modelling" - a term Sam had heard in passing but never fully explored.

Ms. Rivera explained, "Application Threat Modelling is like being a detective. You're trying to think like a hacker to identify and understand the potential threats to your application. It's about asking questions like 'What could go wrong?', 'How likely is it?', and 'What are the potential impacts?'. By understanding these threats, you can build defences against them."

Sam, intrigued, began to see his coding in a new light. He realised that while he had been focused on making the application functional and user-friendly, he hadn't fully considered how a hacker might try to exploit it. Ms. Rivera guided the team through the process of threat modelling, starting with identifying assets that needed protection, like user data and transaction records.

Next, they brainstormed potential threats and vulnerabilities. They considered everything from SQL injections and cross-site scripting to more sophisticated cyber-attacks. Sam was amazed at the variety and complexity of the risks their application could face.

The exercise was an eye-opener for Sam. He understood that building a FinTech application wasn't just about creating features that users would love but also about ensuring these features couldn't be manipulated for malicious purposes. He learned the importance of incorporating security measures from the start, rather than as an afterthought.

Motivated by this newfound knowledge, Sam started integrating security considerations into every phase of the development cycle. He worked closely with Ms. Rivera to implement secure coding practices, set up firewalls, and encrypt sensitive data. Sam also became an advocate for regular security audits and testing, ensuring that the application was not just efficient but also robust and secure.

In the end, the FinTech product was a resounding success. It wasn't just because of its innovative features, but also because users trusted its security. Sam's journey in understanding and implementing Application Threat Modelling played a crucial role in this achievement. He not only grew as a software engineer but also became a champion of cybersecurity in his startup.

From then on, Sam approached every project with a security-first mindset, always remembering that in the digital world, the best offence is a good defence. And so, he continued his journey, coding and securing, in the ever-evolving landscape of technology and cybersecurity.

Sam took the following steps on application threat modelling -

1. Identify and document the assets, data, and functionality of the application.
2. Identify and document the potential threats to these assets, data, and functionality.
3. Identify and document the vulnerabilities that could be exploited by these threats.
4. Identify and document the controls that are currently in place to mitigate these threats and vulnerabilities.
5. Prioritise the threats and vulnerabilities based on their likelihood and impact.
6. Develop and implement a plan to address the most critical threats and vulnerabilities.
7. Continuously monitor and test the application for new threats and vulnerabilities.
8. Update the threat model as the application evolves.

There are different ways to carry out the above steps; one popular method is STRIDE, which is an acronym for Spoofing, Tampering, Repudiation, Information disclosure, Denial of service, Elevation of privilege. This method is used to identify the different types of threats and vulnerabilities that could be present in an application.

It's also important to involve a cross-functional team that includes developers, security experts, and business stakeholders in the threat modelling process to ensure that the results are actionable and aligned with the overall goals of the organisation.

What are the types of authentication used in the applications?

Several types of authentication methods can be used in applications to verify the identity of a user:

1. **Password-based authentication:** This is the most widely used form of authentication, where a user is prompted to enter a username and password to gain access to the application.
2. **Two-factor authentication (2FA):** This type of authentication requires the user to provide two forms of identification, such as a password and a fingerprint or a password and a security token.
3. **Biometric authentication:** This type of authentication uses physical or behavioural characteristics, such as a fingerprint, facial recognition, or voice recognition, to verify the identity of a user.
4. **Token-based authentication:** This type of authentication uses a token or a key to authenticate a user. Tokens can be sent to the user via email or SMS, or can be generated using an app on the user's device.
5. **Certificate-based authentication:** This type of authentication uses digital certificates to verify the identity of a user. Certificates are issued by a trusted third party and contain information about the user's identity.
6. **Multi-factor authentication (MFA)**: This type of authentication requires the user to provide multiple forms of identification, such as a password, a fingerprint, and a security token.
7. **Single sign-on (SSO)**: This type of authentication allows a user to log in to multiple applications using a single set of credentials.

How to use JSON in applications for authentication

JSON Web Tokens (JWTs) are a standard for securely transmitting information between parties. It is often used for authentication and authorisation purposes in web applications. A JWT is a JSON object that is encoded and digitally signed. It consists of three parts: a header, a payload, and a signature. The header typically contains information about the type of token and the signing algorithm used. The payload contains the claims, which are statements about an entity (typically, the user) and additional metadata. The signature is used to verify that the sender of the JWT is who it says it is and to ensure that the message wasn't changed along the way. JWT allows for the transfer of the claims in a compact and self-contained manner, and it is easy to pass them through different systems, such as HTTP headers. This allows the user to authenticate once and then access multiple systems without having to re-authenticate.

JWT tokens are typically used in combination with OAuth2 or OpenID Connect (OIDC) authentication protocols and are often used in RESTful API's, microservices and SPA (Single-Page Applications) as a means of authentication and authorisation. It's important to note that JWT tokens should be stored client-side (e.g., in the browser's local storage) and should be transmitted over an encrypted connection (HTTPS) to prevent eavesdropping and should be validated on the server side before granting access to any protected resources.

Understanding Static Application Security Testing (SAST) for Startups

Static Application Security Testing (SAST) is a method of analysing the source code of a software application to identify security vulnerabilities. SAST tools can scan the code and look for patterns that indicate a potential vulnerability, such as missing input validation, hard-coded credentials, or SQL injection. The goal of SAST is to identify vulnerabilities early in the development process, before the application is deployed, so that they can be addressed and fixed before they can be exploited by attackers.

SAST can be integrated into the software development life cycle (SDLC) and performed automatically as part of the build process. This allows developers to identify and fix vulnerabilities early in the development process when it is less expensive and time-consuming to do so. SAST can be done by developers themselves or by specialised security teams to make sure the code is written securely.

SAST is a great way to find security vulnerabilities in the source code, but it has some limitations. It can only find vulnerabilities that exist in the source code and cannot identify vulnerabilities that may be introduced by the configuration of the application or the underlying infrastructure. It also can't find vulnerabilities that are only exploitable during runtime. To have more comprehensive security coverage, it's recommended to use SAST in conjunction with other testing methodologies such as DAST (Dynamic Application Security Testing) and IAST (Interactive Application Security Testing).

What is DAST, and how to carry out DAST?

DAST stands for Dynamic Application Security Testing. It is a technique used to identify security vulnerabilities in web applications and APIs by actively interacting with the application and sending various inputs to it to detect any weaknesses or vulnerabilities in the system. DAST tools can be used to scan for common vulnerabilities such as SQL injection, cross- site scripting (XSS), and insecure file uploads, among others.

There are several steps involved in carrying out a Dynamic Application Security Test (DAST):

1. **Planning**: Before starting the test, it is important to plan the scope of the test, identify the target systems and applications, and determine the goals and objectives of the test.
2. **Configuration**: Next, the DAST tool needs to be configured to suit the specific needs of the test. This includes setting up the target systems, configuring the test settings, and selecting the appropriate test methods and techniques.
3. **Execution**: The DAST test is then executed by actively interacting with the target application and sending various inputs to it to detect any vulnerabilities or weaknesses.
4. **Analysis**: Once the test is completed, the results are analysed to identify any vulnerabilities that were found. This includes reviewing the test results, identifying any false positives or negatives, and

determining the severity of any vulnerabilities that were discovered.

5. **Reporting:** Finally, a detailed report is prepared that includes the results of the test, any vulnerabilities that were found, and recommendations for remediation.

It's important to note that DAST is one of the many ways to test the security of a web application, and it should be combined with other testing techniques such as SAST, Penetration Testing and manual testing.

Cloud Security: Secure your cloud before it bursts.

The Growing Importance of Cloud Security

In today's digital age, the proliferation of cloud computing has transformed the way businesses operate, enabling agility, scalability, and cost-efficiency. As organisations increasingly migrate their operations and data to the cloud, the importance of robust cloud security measures has grown exponentially. Cloud security is not just a matter of safeguarding data; it's a fundamental pillar of trust, continuity, and regulatory compliance.

Firstly, data breaches have become a ubiquitous threat, with cybercriminals constantly evolving their tactics to exploit vulnerabilities in cloud infrastructure. The sheer volume of sensitive information stored in the cloud, ranging from customer data to intellectual property, makes it an attractive target. Therefore, organisations must implement rigorous access controls, encryption protocols, and continuous monitoring to protect their data from unauthorised access and data breaches. The reputational damage, financial losses, and legal consequences that can result from a breach underscore the critical nature of cloud security.

Secondly, regulatory bodies around the world have introduced stringent data protection and privacy laws, such as the General Data Protection Regulation (GDPR) and the California Consumer Privacy Act (CCPA). These regulations impose strict requirements on how organisations handle and secure data, with severe penalties for non-compliance. Cloud service providers and their customers share the responsibility for complying with these regulations, emphasising the need for a robust security framework that includes data encryption, identity and access management, and auditing capabilities.

Lastly, the cloud has become the foundation for digital innovation, enabling businesses to embrace emerging technologies like artificial intelligence, Internet of Things (IoT), and big data analytics. While these technologies offer tremendous opportunities, they also introduce new security challenges. Protecting cloud-based resources from advanced threats and vulnerabilities is essential to ensure the integrity of these innovative solutions. As businesses continue to rely on the cloud as their technological cornerstone, investing in cloud security has become not just a priority but a strategic imperative to maintain a competitive edge and safeguard against evolving cyber threats.

One of the primary drivers of this intersection is the rapid pace of technological innovation. Emerging technologies like artificial intelligence (AI), the Internet of Things (IoT), and quantum computing have the potential to revolutionise industries and improve efficiency, but they also introduce novel security challenges. For example, AI can be used by both cybercriminals and cybersecurity experts, creating a constant battle of wits. IoT devices, while enhancing connectivity, often lack robust security measures, making them vulnerable to exploitation. Quantum computing threatens current encryption methods, necessitating the development of quantum-resistant cryptography. Keeping pace with these technological advances and their associated threats is a constant challenge for cybersecurity professionals.

Another factor contributing to this intersection is the increasing digital interconnectedness of our world. The proliferation of connected devices, cloud computing, and the expansion of digital ecosystems have created a vast attack surface for cybercriminals. As more data and critical infrastructure move online, the potential impact of cyberattacks has grown exponentially. Nation-states, criminal organisations, and lone hackers are all drawn to the vast troves of data and potential disruptions that can result from exploiting vulnerabilities in interconnected systems. Protecting against these threats requires not only strong cybersecurity measures but also international cooperation and information sharing to stay one step ahead of cyber adversaries.

Moreover, the sophistication of cyber threats continues to rise. Attackers use advanced techniques such as social engineering, zero-day vulnerabilities, and polymorphic malware to evade detection and compromise systems. The intersection of technology advancements and cyber threats means that traditional security approaches are no longer sufficient. Organisations must adopt a proactive and adaptive cybersecurity strategy that includes threat intelligence, machine learning, and continuous monitoring to identify and respond to emerging threats in real-time.

Artificial Intelligence (AI) and Machine Learning (ML) have emerged as game-changers in various domains, including cybersecurity. While AI and ML can be used to enhance threat detection and automate security responses, they can also be harnessed by cybercriminals to create more sophisticated and evasive attacks. For example, AI-driven malware can adapt its behaviour in real-time to evade detection, posing a significant challenge to traditional security measures. Staying ahead of these AI-powered threats require cybersecurity professionals to employ AI and ML in their defensive strategies while continually refining their models to counter evolving tactics.

The cloud has become the backbone of modern IT infrastructure, enabling businesses to scale rapidly and reduce operational costs. However, the shift to cloud-based environments has introduced a new set of security concerns. These include misconfigurations of cloud services, inadequate access controls, and the potential for data exposure due to human error. Startups must adapt their security practices to the cloud- native paradigm, embracing tools and practices that ensure the secure configuration and monitoring of cloud resources.

Additionally, the evolving threat landscape is marked by the increasing sophistication of nation-state actors and organised cybercrime groups. These entities possess significant resources and expertise, allowing them to launch highly targeted and persistent attacks on critical infrastructure, government institutions, and corporations. State-sponsored cyber-espionage and cyber-attacks on critical infrastructure, such as power grids and water systems, have become ominous threats that necessitate international cooperation and concerted efforts to bolster defences.

As enterprises start moving towards cloud computing platforms like Amazon AWS, Google Cloud, and Azure, it is essential to understand cloud security compliance. Cloud security is all about securing your data in the cloud from data theft, unauthorised access, data leaks, etc.

In this chapter, we explore the intricacies of cloud security, focusing on its various components and essential strategies for ensuring robust protection in cloud environments. We will also examine best practices and methodologies to effectively implement and maintain cloud security measures. The chapter aims to provide startups with a comprehensive understanding of cloud security, covering everything from fundamental principles to advanced protective techniques.

1) What is Cloud Security?

Cloud security encompasses the measures and protocols put in place to safeguard data and assets hosted in cloud environments. This comprehensive approach includes the protection of data during transmission, storage, and utilisation, as well as the security of cloud-based applications and systems. Ensuring robust cloud security is of paramount importance, particularly for organisations that rely on cloud services.

The inherent characteristic of shared infrastructure in the cloud amplifies security concerns. Data and resources coexist on servers utilised by multiple users, making them potentially more susceptible to security breaches compared to a traditional on-premises setup.

2) Pillars of Cloud Security

The pillars of cloud security encompass the fundamental principles and areas of focus for ensuring the security of cloud-based environments. Here are the key pillars of cloud security, presented in a point-wise manner:

1. **Identity and Access Management (IAM)** plays a critical role in ensuring the security of cloud environments. It encompasses several key components and practices that collectively help organisations manage user access, authenticate users, and control permissions to safeguard their cloud resources. Here's an expansion of the elements within IAM:

Centralised User Authentication and Authorisation:

- ❖ Centralised IAM systems serve as the gatekeepers for accessing cloud resources. They authenticate the identity of users or entities attempting to access services.
- ❖ User identities are verified through various means, including usernames and passwords, tokens, or biometric data.
- ❖ Authorisation policies define what actions or resources each authenticated user or entity is allowed to access within the cloud environment.
- ❖ IAM solutions ensure that only authorised users or services can interact with cloud resources, reducing the risk of unauthorised access.

Role-Based Access Control (RBAC):

- ❖ RBAC is a key principle within IAM that enhances security by providing fine-grained control over permissions.
- ❖ Users and entities are assigned roles, which define their access privileges within the cloud ecosystem. Roles can include administrators, developers, and read-only users, among others.
- ❖ Permissions associated with each role are carefully defined, ensuring that users have the least privilege necessary to perform their tasks. This minimises the risk of users accessing or modifying resources beyond their scope.
- ❖ RBAC simplifies access management, scalability, and compliance by organising permissions based on roles rather than individual users.

Multi-Factor Authentication (MFA):

- ❖ MFA is a powerful security measure that adds layer of protection to user authentication.
- ❖ In addition to traditional username and password combinations, MFA requires users to provide a second form of authentication, such as a one-time code sent to their mobile device or a fingerprint scan.

- MFA significantly enhances identity verification by ensuring that even if an attacker gains access to a user's credentials, they still cannot access the account without the second authentication factor.
- This robust authentication method is particularly crucial for securing sensitive accounts and resources within the cloud, as it greatly reduces the risk of unauthorised access due to compromised passwords.

3) Data Protection:

For startups, data protection is crucial to safeguarding sensitive information, maintaining customer trust, and ensuring compliance with regulations. Startups must implement strong encryption practices for data both at rest and in transit, utilise secure backups, and establish stringent access controls. Educating employees about data security and implementing robust monitoring systems can help detect and mitigate potential breaches. By prioritising data protection, startups can build a secure foundation that supports growth and fosters trust with their clients and stakeholders.

Encryption of Data at Rest and in Transit in the Cloud

1) Data at Rest Encryption:

Purpose: To protect stored data from unauthorised access, especially important in cloud storage where data resides in shared infrastructure.

Techniques:

- Encryption of files on cloud storage services.
- Use of encrypted volumes for cloud-based virtual machines.
- Employing encryption services provided by cloud vendors like AWS S3 encryption, Azure Storage Service Encryption, or Google Cloud's Persistent Disk encryption.

Key Considerations:

- Choosing an appropriate encryption algorithm (e.g., AES-256).
- Managing performance impacts, as encryption can increase resource usage.

2) Data in Transit Encryption:

Purpose: To secure data as it moves between cloud services, users, and other networks, protecting it from interception or alteration.

Techniques:

- Implementing SSL/TLS protocols for secure data transmission.
- Utilising VPNs (Virtual Private Networks) for additional security layers.
- Ensuring APIs and endpoints used in cloud services are secured with HTTPS.

Key Considerations:

- Regularly updating encryption protocols to avoid vulnerabilities.
- Balancing encryption strength with latency and speed requirements.

Robust Key Management for Cryptographic Keys

1. **Importance of Cloud:** Key management is crucial in the cloud due to the distributed nature of services and the shared responsibility model of cloud security.
2. **Best Practices:**
   - **Centralised Management:** Using cloud-based key management services like AWS KMS, Azure Key Vault, or Google Cloud KMS.
   - **Access Control:** Strictly controlling who has access to keys and under what conditions.
   - **Rotation and Backup**: Regularly rotating keys and keeping secure backups.
   - **Audit and Compliance:** Maintaining comprehensive audit logs for key access and usage to ensure compliance with regulatory standards.

Data Loss Prevention (DLP) Mechanisms in the Cloud

Purpose: DLP mechanisms help prevent unintentional loss or unauthorised access to sensitive data.

Implementation in Cloud:

- **Cloud DLP Solutions:** Implementing DLP solutions offered by cloud providers or third-party solutions integrated into the cloud environment.
- **Data Classification**: Classifying data based on sensitivity and applying DLP policies accordingly.
- **Monitoring and Alerts**: Continuously monitoring data movement and access, with alerts for suspicious activities or policy violations.

Key Considerations:

- **Policy Customisation**: Creating DLP policies that reflect the specific needs and compliance requirements of the organisation.
- **Integration with Other Security Tools:** Ensuring DLP solutions work cohesively with encryption, IAM, and other security systems.

3. **Network Security:** encompasses various practices and technologies designed to protect the integrity and usability of networks and data. Here's an expanded view of the three components you mentioned:

1) Network Segmentation to Isolate Workloads:

Purpose: Network segmentation involves dividing a network into smaller, more manageable parts to enhance security and performance. Each segment contains a specific group of devices or resources, creating isolated environments.

Benefits:

- **Enhanced Security:** Isolating segments ensures that if one is compromised, the breach doesn’t spread to other parts of the network.

- **Improved Performance:** Reduces network congestion by limiting unnecessary traffic between segments.
- **Easier Troubleshooting:** Simplifies the process of identifying and resolving network issues.

Implementation:

- **Physical Segmentation:** Uses separate hardware for different network layers.
- **Virtual Segmentation (VLANs):** Creates virtual networks within a physical network.
- **Software-Defined Networking (SDN):** Provides a dynamic, manageable, and cost-effective network environment.

Illustration: Consider a start-up office network as a series of islands. Physical segmentation is like building separate bridges to each island, VLANs are akin to creating invisible borders on the same island, and SDN is like having flexible, automated pathways that adjust to the traffic needs. By isolating workloads through these methods, a start-up can maintain secure and efficient network operations.

2) Firewalls and Intrusion Detection/Prevention Systems (IDS/IPS): Firewalls serve as a crucial barrier between a trusted network and the untrusted internet, ensuring only authorised traffic passes through. There are two main types: network firewalls, which filter traffic for an entire network, and host-based firewalls, which provide more detailed control by being installed on individual devices.

In addition to firewalls, Intrusion Detection Systems (IDS) and Intrusion Prevention Systems (IPS) play a vital role in network security. IDS monitors network traffic for suspicious activity and alerts administrators, while IPS actively prevents or blocks intrusions in real-time. Both can be deployed at the network level to protect entire systems or at the host level for individual device security.

The primary benefits of these systems include preventing unauthorised access and detecting and responding to threats effectively. By setting security rules, firewalls limit access, while IDS/IPS identify and can automatically counter potential threats, creating a robust security framework for startups.

Illustration: Imagine a medieval castle with two lines of defence—the outer walls (network firewalls) guard the entire perimeter, while the inner guards (host-based firewalls) protect individual rooms. Meanwhile, vigilant sentinels (IDS) watch for any suspicious activity, ready to alert the guards, and trained defenders (IPS) stand by to repel any intruders in real-time.

3) Monitoring and Control of Network Traffic:

To effectively oversee and manage the flow of data in and out of the network, startups must employ several key methods and tools. Traffic analysis involves examining data packets to detect anomalies or unauthorised activity, while bandwidth management regulates network resources to prevent overuse or misuse. Essential tools for this purpose include network monitoring software, which provides real-time insights into network performance and security, and protocol analysers for deep packet inspection and analysis. The benefits of these methods are significant: they offer clear visibility into network operations, help in the early detection of security breaches, and optimise network performance by identifying and resolving issues. Together, these components form a robust framework for network security, safeguarding against various cyber threats while ensuring the network runs smoothly and efficiently.

Illustration: A diagram showing network monitoring tools and protocol analysers at work, highlighting the flow of data and how anomalies are detected and managed.

4. **Incident Response and Recovery** in a cloud environment involves a set of procedures and tools designed to promptly detect, respond to, and recover from security incidents or disruptions.

Efficient incident detection and response plans are crucial for start-ups to identify and address security incidents within cloud environments. These plans encompass several key elements:

Preparation involves establishing a dedicated response team, defining roles and responsibilities, and training staff. **Identification** leverages monitoring tools to detect anomalies and potential threats. **Containment**

focuses on isolating affected systems to prevent the spread of an incident. **Eradication** entails removing the cause of the incident and securing the environment, while **Recovery** restores systems and data to normal operations. Finally, **Post-Incident Analysis** reviews the incident to improve future responses and prevent recurrence.

Start-ups face unique challenges in cloud environments, such as navigating the **Shared Responsibility Model**, which defines the division of security tasks between the cloud provider and the user. Additionally, they must adapt to the **Dynamic and Scalable Nature** of cloud resources.

Automated Incident Response Tools play a pivotal role in enhancing detection and response efforts. Tools like **Security Information and Event Management (SIEM)** provide real-time analysis of security alerts, while **Security Orchestration, Automation, and Response (SOAR)** integrates various security solutions and automates workflows. These tools offer benefits including rapid response, consistent procedures, and reduced workload for security teams. However, considerations such as seamless integration with existing cloud services and customisation to specific cloud environments and organisational policies are essential for effective implementation.

Illustration: Imagine a start-up cloud infrastructure as a castle under constant threat. The incident response team are the knights, with specific roles and a well-rehearsed plan. Monitoring tools act as sentinels, detecting intruders. When a breach occurs, affected areas are swiftly contained (drawbridges raised), threats eradicated (intruders expelled), and normal operations restored (castle life resumes). Automated tools serve as vigilant allies, ensuring rapid, uniform responses and easing the burden on the knights. This fortress analogy underscores the importance of a comprehensive, prepared approach to cloud security.

5. Backup and Disaster Recovery Strategies:

To safeguard data and services in the event of a disaster or data loss incident, startups must focus on effective data protection strategies. Key components include regular backups, where data is saved to secure, separate locations, and disaster recovery (DR) planning, which ensures the rapid restoration of disrupted services and data. Implementing redundancy by storing backups in multiple locations, including off-site or in different cloud regions, is vital. Regular testing of backups and recovery processes, alongside defining Recovery Time Objectives (RTO) and Recovery Point Objectives (RPO) for critical data and systems, helps maintain readiness. Startups should also consider cloud-specific factors, leveraging the cloud's scalability for cost-effective backup storage and understanding backup and DR responsibilities across different cloud service models such as IaaS, PaaS, and SaaS.

6. **Visibility and monitoring** in cloud environments are crucial for maintaining operational efficiency and security. These practices involve real-time monitoring of cloud resources, log management and analysis, and integrating Security Information and Event Management (SIEM) systems. Each major cloud provider, such as Google Cloud Platform (GCP), Amazon Web Services (AWS), and Microsoft Azure, offers tools and services to facilitate these processes. Here's a detailed look:

Real-Time Monitoring of Cloud Resources:

The purpose of monitoring cloud resources is to continuously observe their performance, availability, and security. Implementation varies across different cloud platforms. Google Cloud's Operations Suite (formerly Stackdriver) offers monitoring, logging, and diagnostics, enabling real-time tracking of resource usage, alert setup, and metric visualisation. Amazon CloudWatch provides real-time monitoring for AWS resources and applications, offering metrics for CPU utilisation, network activity, and customizable dashboards. Azure Monitor collects and analyses telemetry data from both Azure and on-premises environments, featuring application monitoring, infrastructure monitoring, and network performance monitoring capabilities.

Log Management and Analysis:

The primary purpose of collecting, storing, and analysing log data is to aid in troubleshooting, enhance security, and ensure compliance. Different cloud platforms offer various tools for this task. Google Cloud Platform (GCP) uses Google Cloud Logging, part of its Operations Suite, to collect, analyse, and export logs from Google Cloud services and virtual machines (VMs). Amazon Web Services (AWS) employs AWS CloudTrail to track user activity and API usage, Amazon CloudWatch Logs to collect and monitor log files, and the AWS Elasticsearch Service for log analytics. Microsoft Azure offers Azure Log Analytics within Azure Monitor, which gathers and analyses data from both Azure resources and on-premises environments. These tools are integral for maintaining robust operational health and security in startup environments.

Security Information and Event Management (SIEM) Integration: The purpose of this section is to provide an in-depth analysis of security alerts generated by applications and network hardware. Implementation varies across different cloud platforms. In GCP, integration with SIEM tools is achieved by exporting logs and metrics from the Operations Suite to external SIEM solutions for advanced analysis. AWS offers seamless integration with popular SIEM tools like Splunk and IBM QRadar, and AWS Security Hub provides a comprehensive view of security alerts. Azure features Azure Sentinel, a cloud-native SIEM solution that delivers intelligent security analytics across enterprise environments and integrates with various sources, including other cloud platforms.

7. **Security by Design for Cloud,** DevOps, and DevSecOps involves embedding security principles and practices into the entire development and operational lifecycle. This approach ensures that security is not an afterthought but an integral part of the development, deployment, and maintenance processes. Here's an expanded view of the components you mentioned, including the integration of security using Jenkins and other open-source Descopes tools:

Integration of Security into the Development Lifecycle Using Descopes:

Descopes integrates security within the DevOps process, automating core security tasks by embedding controls early in the development cycle. This includes a "Shift Left" approach to consider security from the start, writing security into code, and embedding security tools into CI/CD workflows. Tools like Jenkins automate security scans, while SonarQube and Terraform help maintain secure code and infrastructure.

Secure Configurations and Templates for Cloud Resources:

To ensure cloud resources are secure from the outset, use Infrastructure as Code (IaC) tools like Terraform or AWS CloudFormation, and configuration management tools like Ansible, Chef, or Puppet. This approach standardises configurations, reducing misconfigurations, and automates secure infrastructure deployment, improving efficiency and accuracy.

Continuous Security Assessment and Remediation:

Continuous security assessment involves identifying and addressing vulnerabilities using automated tools like OWASP ZAP and Nessus, and real-time monitoring with Prometheus or Elastic Stack. Integrate these tools into CI/CD pipelines using Jenkins to run security assessments during deployment, ensuring security issues are promptly addressed.

Integrating Security Using Jenkins and Other Open Source Descopes Tools:

Jenkins automates security integration at various stages of software delivery, using plugins for static and dynamic code analysis. Integrate Jenkins pipelines to include security scanning and reporting. Other tools like SonarQube, Docker, and GitLab CI/CD also support continuous security scanning and secure container deployment.

8. **Ensuring cloud security through contractual agreements** with cloud providers is a critical aspect of cloud management. It involves a clear understanding, documentation, and legal commitments regarding security responsibilities, compliance, data protection, and other security-related aspects. Here are key steps and considerations for managing cloud security contractually with cloud providers:

1) **Understand the Shared Responsibility Model:**

   - ❖ **Definition**: Cloud security involves a shared responsibility model. The cloud provider secures the infrastructure, while the customer secures their data within it.
   - ❖ **Implication**: Clearly define security responsibilities in contracts.

2) **Specify Security Requirements and Standards:**

   - ❖ Requirements: Set specific security requirements like encryption standards and access controls.
   - ❖ Compliance: Ensure the provider meets industry and regulatory

standards (e.g., GDPR, HIPAA, PCI DSS).

3) **Data Management and Protection:**

- **Data Location**: Specify where data will be stored to comply with data sovereignty laws.
- **Data Access:** Define access controls and conditions.
- **Data Encryption**: Ensure policies for encrypting data in transit and at rest.

4) **Incident Response and Reporting:**

- **Incident Response:** Detail the cloud provider's responsibilities during a security breach, including notifications and response times.
- **Reporting**: Require regular security reports and audits.

5) **Audit Rights and Compliance Certifications:**

- **Audit Rights:** Negotiate rights for independent security audits.
- **Certifications**: Require the provider to maintain certifications like ISO 27001 and SOC 2.

6) **Service Level Agreements (SLAs) and Penalties:**

- **SLAs**: Define security-related SLAs, including uptime and support response times.
- **Penalties**: Include penalties for SLA breaches or security failures.

7) **End-of-Contract and Data Portability:**

- **Data Retrieval:** Ensure terms for data retrieval at contract end or termination.
- **Data Deletion**: Set policies for data deletion post-contract to prevent unauthorised access.

8) **Regular Review and Updates:**

- **Dynamic Nature**: Acknowledge that cloud services and compliance need change, requiring regular contract updates.
- **Review Schedule:** Schedule regular contract reviews and

amendments.

9) **Legal and Regulatory Considerations:**

- **Legal Expertise**: Consult legal experts in technology and cloud contracts to cover all regulatory aspects.
- **Jurisdiction**: Understand the legal jurisdiction governing the contract and its impact on dispute resolution.

10) **Negotiation and Customisation:**

- **Negotiation**: Be ready to negotiate terms to meet specific security needs.
- **Customisation:** Tailor the contract to address t h e unique risks and requirements of your startup.

Addressing these areas in contracts with cloud providers enhances cloud security and ensures critical security aspects are covered.

9. **User education and awareness**, particularly in the context of cloud security, are essential components of a robust cybersecurity strategy. For DevOps engineers and other IT professionals, being knowledgeable about security best practices, emerging threats, and effective countermeasures in cloud environments is vital. Here's how DevOps engineers can stay informed and aware:

Understanding Security in DevOps:

- **Security Integration:** Security is part of the entire DevOps process, not a separate phase.
- **Security by Design:** Consider security at every step of software development and operations.

Continuous Learning and Training:

- **Education:** Enroll in cybersecurity courses on cloud security from universities or online platforms.
- **Certifications:** Obtain certifications like AWS Certified Security-Speciality, Microsoft Certified: Azure Security Engineer Associate, or Google Cloud's Professional Cloud Security Engineer.

Online Resources and Communities:

- **Blogs and Forums:** Follow reputable blogs and forums on cloud security and DevOps, such as DevOps.com and Cloud Security Alliance.
- **Webinars and Workshops:** Attend webinars and online workshops by cloud service providers or cybersecurity firms.

Workshops and Conferences:

- **Industry Conferences:** Attend conferences like AWS re, Microsoft Ignite, and Google Cloud Next.
- **Hands-On Workshops:** Participate in workshops for practical experience in cloud security.

Leveraging Cloud Provider Resources:

- **Documentation:** Use documentation, whitepapers, and best practice guides from AWS, Azure, and GCP.
- **Training Programs:** Engage with training programs that include security modules.

Interactive Learning Platforms:

- **Courses:** Use platforms like Coursera, Udemy, or Pluralsight for cloud security and DevOps courses.
- **Interactive Labs:** Practice with hands-on labs from A Cloud Guru, Linux Academy, or Qwiklabs.

Staying Updated:

- **Newsletters:** Subscribe to newsletters from cybersecurity and cloud computing outlets.
- **Security Researchers:** Follow renowned security researchers on social media or blogs.

Internal Training and Knowledge Sharing:

- **Training Sessions:** Organise regular training sessions within your organisation.

- **Knowledge Sharing:** Engage in sessions to discuss new findings and best practices.

Security Communities and Groups:

- **Online Communities:** Join forums like Stack Overflow, Reddit's r/devops, or r/cloud security.
- **Professional Groups:** Join groups like ISACA, (ISC)², or local cybersecurity groups.

Practical Experience:

- **Simulated Environments:** Practice in simulated cloud environments to understand security configurations.
- **CTF Challenges:** Participate in Capture the Flag challenges focused on cloud security.

For developers, staying educated and aware in the field of cloud security is an ongoing process. It involves actively seeking knowledge, engaging with the community, and continuously applying and updating skills in practical scenarios.

These pillars serve as a framework for organisations to build a comprehensive and resilient cloud security strategy. By addressing each of these areas, businesses can establish a strong foundation for safeguarding their cloud-based resources and data.

3. Benefits of Cloud Security

The adoption of cloud security offers numerous benefits to organisations, enhancing not only their security posture but also their operational efficiency and cost-effectiveness.

3.1 Cost Savings

- **Reduced Capital Expenditure:** Cloud security minimises the need for investment in physical security infrastructure like servers and hardware, shifting from a capital expenditure model to an operational one.
- **Pay-As-You-Go Model:** Many cloud security services operate on a pay-as-you-go basis, allowing businesses to pay only for the

services and capacity they need.

- **Reduced Maintenance Costs:** Cloud providers typically handle maintenance, updates, and patches, reducing the internal IT workload and associated costs.
- **Scalability:** The ability to scale services up or down based on demand ensures that companies don't overpay for unused capacity.
- **No Need for Physical Space:** Eliminating the need for physical space for servers can result in significant savings in terms of real estate and utility costs.

3.2 Increased Efficiency

- **Automated Updates and Maintenance:** Cloud security providers regularly update and maintain their systems, ensuring that the latest security measures are in place without additional effort from the user.
- **Rapid Deployment:** Cloud services can be deployed much faster than traditional on-premises solutions, enabling quicker response to evolving business needs.
- **Enhanced Flexibility:** Cloud security offers greater flexibility, allowing employees to securely access data and applications from anywhere, which is particularly beneficial for remote or distributed workforces.
- **Centralised Management:** Centralised management of security policies and procedures in the cloud simplifies the control of data and applications across multiple locations.

3.3 Better Protection

- **Advanced Security Features:** Cloud providers typically offer advanced security features, including encryption, intrusion detection, and identity management.
- **Regular Security Updates:** Continuous security updates help in protecting against the latest threats without the need for manual intervention.

- **Disaster Recovery and Redundancy:** Cloud services often include robust disaster recovery capabilities and data redundancy, ensuring data integrity and availability even in the event of a system failure or cyber-attack.
- **Economies of Scale:** Cloud providers can leverage economies of scale to offer high-level security features that might be cost-prohibitive for individual organisations to implement on their own.
- **Compliance and Standards:** Cloud providers often adhere to a variety of compliance standards and regulations, providing an additional layer of security assurance.

Additional Considerations

- **Customizable Security Solutions:** Cloud security can be tailored to the specific needs of a business, providing customised protection.
- **Access to Expertise:** By using cloud services, organisations have access to the expertise and advanced technologies of cloud providers.
- **Proactive Threat Monitoring:** Cloud services often include proactive monitoring, which can detect and respond to threats more quickly than traditional methods.

In conclusion, cloud security offers a compelling blend of cost savings, increased efficiency, and enhanced protection. These benefits make it an attractive option for organisations of all sizes, looking to improve their security posture while also optimising operational and cost efficiencies.

4. Critical Security Threats

When it comes to securing your AWS (Amazon Web Services) environment, it's crucial to cover various components to ensure comprehensive protection. Below are key areas to focus on:

- **Perimeter Security:** Implement strong security measures at the perimeter of your AWS infrastructure to prevent unauthorised access.

- **Edge Servers:** Secure edge servers and endpoints to protect against external threats and ensure secure communication.
- **Network Security:** Configure network security settings, such as firewalls and security groups, to control traffic and prevent unauthorised access.
- **Containers:** Secure containerised applications using best practices such as image scanning, runtime protection, and access controls.
- **API Security:** Protect APIs from attacks and misuse by implementing authentication, authorisation, and rate limiting.
- **Compliance:** Ensure compliance with relevant regulations and standards to maintain data security and privacy.
- **Data Security (Privacy):** Implement measures to protect sensitive data, including encryption, access controls, and data masking.
- **Identity Management:** Manage user identities and permissions effectively to prevent unauthorised access to AWS resources.
- **Encryption:** Encrypt data at rest and in transit using AWS encryption services to protect against data breaches.

To illustrate further, imagine your AWS infrastructure as a fortress. The perimeter acts as sturdy walls guarding against intruders. Edge servers are like watchtowers, monitoring incoming threats. Network security forms the gates controlling who can enter and exit. Containers are secure compartments within the fortress, protecting valuable assets. APIs are like secret passages, accessible only to authorized individuals. Compliance standards ensure the fortress meets regulations. Data security safeguards treasure chests of information. Identity management controls who can enter the fortress, and encryption keeps secrets safe from prying eyes.

4.1 AWS Cloud

Amazon AWS stands as a leader in the cloud computing arena, being a key provider for prominent companies like Facebook, Netflix, and Twitch, thanks to its reliable performance. AWS offers a range of efficient tools and robust default security configurations.

However, AWS users face several security challenges, including:

- **Unauthorised Cloud Data Access**: Risk of external parties accessing cloud-stored data without authorisation.
- **Insecure Interfaces and APIs**: Potential breaches stemming from unprotected user interfaces and APIs, often targeted first by cybercriminals.
- **Compromised Accounts**: The danger of account hacking due to insufficient account protection.
- **Misconfigured AWS Firewall Manager**: Incorrect configuration settings can leave the network vulnerable.
- **Improper IAM (Identity and Access Management) Controls Management**: Mishandling IAM controls can lead to unauthorised access and security breaches.

Additionally, certain AWS features, if misconfigured or mishandled, can pose security threats:

- **Amazon S3 Server Access Logging**: By default, S3 servers have logging turned off. Activating logging incurs no extra charges, but storing log files does. Without logging, it's challenging to track data requests and access details.
- **Database Security in Cloud Computing**: With data shared among various SaaS providers, each having different access levels, encryption is crucial to prevent unauthorised access. The security effectiveness in a multi-tenancy environment largely depends on the robustness of the implemented security measures.
- **Key Management Challenges**: Proper generation, storage, and renewal of encryption keys are vital. Any lapses can lead to keys being compromised, risking data loss or theft.
- **EC2 and EBS Security Limitations**: While offering general security, EC2 and EBS don't restrict data access within AWS

instances by default. Implementing strict rules and policies for data decryption at the file system level is necessary.

- **AWS Inspector**: This tool helps identify vulnerable resources, potential exploit likelihoods, and deviations from security best practices. It also aids in understanding the root causes of potential security issues, allowing for proactive mitigation.
- **AWS Guard Duty**: This service analyses data across AWS accounts and services to detect threats, enhancing overall security posture.

Unauthorised Access to Cloud Data:

- **Nature of Threat**: This involves external entities gaining access to sensitive data stored on AWS without proper authorisation.
- **Mitigation Strategies**: Implementing strong access controls, using multi-factor authentication, and ensuring that IAM policies are correctly configured to grant the least privilege necessary.

Security Vulnerabilities from Unsecured Interfaces and APIs:

- **Nature of Threat**: APIs and interfaces that lack robust security measures can be exploited by attackers to gain unauthorised access or disrupt services.
- **Mitigation Strategies**: Regularly auditing and testing APIs for vulnerabilities, implementing API gateways with strong authentication and encryption, and adhering to best practices in API security.

Compromised Account Security:

- **Nature of Threat**: Attackers may gain access to AWS accounts through phishing, brute force attacks, or exploiting weak credentials.
- **Mitigation Strategies**: Enforcing strong password policies, educating users about phishing and other social engineering attacks, and monitoring for unusual account activity that could indicate a compromise.

Incorrect Configuration of AWS Firewall Manager:

- **Nature of Threat**: Misconfigured firewall settings can leave the AWS environment exposed to potential attacks or data breaches.
- **Mitigation Strategies**: Regularly reviewing and auditing firewall configurations, using automated tools to detect misconfigurations, and training staff on correct firewall setup and maintenance.

Improper Management of IAM (Identity and Access Management) Controls:

- **Nature of Threat**: Inadequate management of IAM can lead to excessive permissions, unauthorized access, and potential security breaches.
- **Mitigation Strategies**: Regularly reviewing IAM roles and policies, implementing principle of least privilege, and conducting periodic audits to ensure that IAM configurations align with the organization's security policies.

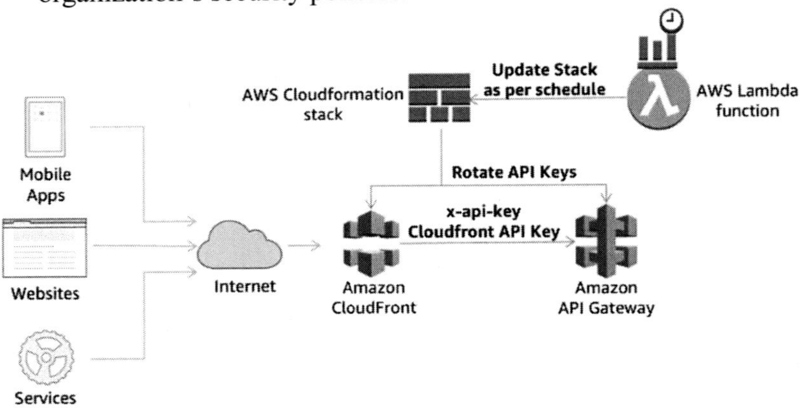

Fig. (1.0) - AWS API Security

- **Improper Configuration of Amazon CloudTrail**

With Amazon CloudTrail, users will know all the API requests made, so it is essential to have CloudTrail enabled. Without CloudTrail, you never will have information about who, when, or where accessed your data.

With CloudTrail enabled, admins can ensure that every API call is recorded, whether it comes from a customer, SaaS application, or another AWS service. Any improper configuration or failure to create a CloudTrail will leave the AWS account owners cold after a security breach.

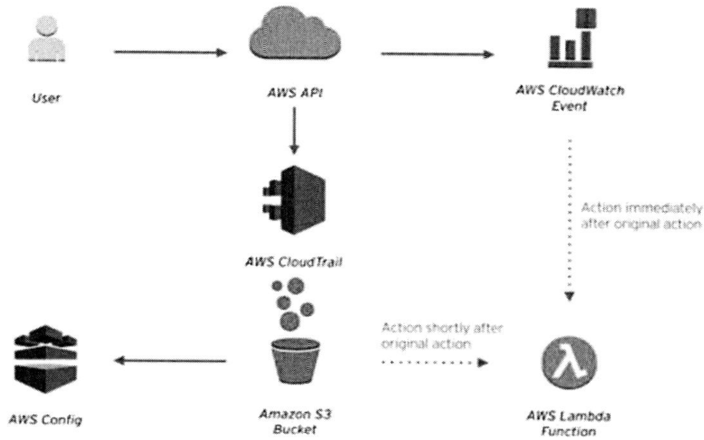

Fig. (2.0) - AWS Cloud Security

4.2 Microsoft Azure

Azure, Microsoft's renowned cloud computing platform, is designed to assist organisations in developing, testing, deploying, and managing applications via Microsoft-managed data centres. Offering a versatile range of services, including Infrastructure as a Service (IaaS), Software as a Service (SaaS), and Platform as a Service (PaaS), Azure caters to a broad spectrum of programming languages and tools, accommodating diverse development needs.

Below is a list of security challenges identified in the Azure platform:

- **Identity-Based Protection**

While Microsoft provides several identity tools for Identify and Access Management, it differs from the level of management offered by AWS or Google Cloud. Hence, it is better to use other identity management tools like Bitglass for enhanced identity management.

- **Security Policy**

By default, several key configurations are set to OFF. These need to be enabled to ensure that the virtual machines in the cloud are safe and receive alerts quickly. Some of the basic configurations that need to be set to ON are:

- OS Vulnerabilities
- Endpoint Protection
- JIT Network Access

For example, turning on Endpoint protection allows Azure to automatically identify and eliminate all kinds of spyware, malware, and viruses in the cloud.

- **Data Security**

Cloud security is often considered a shared responsibility model, and with Microsoft Azure, it is much more. With Azure, it is the responsibility of the IaaS users to take responsibility for the security of the database and other applications installed.

Any MySQL or MongoDB installed in Azure need to be adequately secured for data security. There are many cases where records have been stolen or leaked due to misconfiguration of security settings in the database.

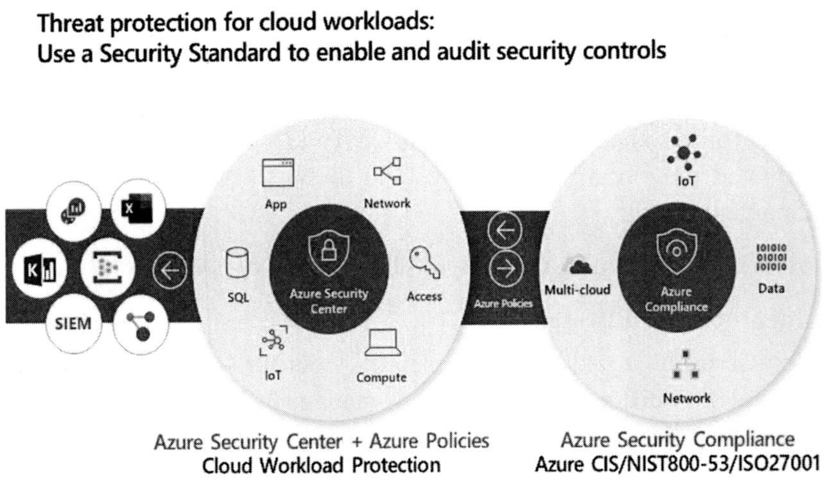

Fig (3.0) Azure Security Compliance

Azure also lacks an advanced alert and notification system, so security vulnerabilities may remain hidden from your eyes until a significant issue happens. Also, data encryption is very straightforward with Azure, and it is always recommended to have your data encrypted at rest.

- **Cloud Misconfiguration**

One of the significant root causes of security issues with Azure is the misconfiguration of the cloud. Even though Azure is highly secure, it is easy to misconfigure things instantly.

4.3 Google Cloud

Google's history, marked by extensive experience in countering cyberattacks, has significantly influenced the development of its Google Cloud Platform. This expertise is deeply integrated into the platform's architecture, ensuring a high level of safety and security for users. However, given that hackers and adversaries continually evolve their tactics to breach data defences, it's crucial to maintain constant vigilance and not become complacent regarding cloud security. Let's take a look at some of the security compliance issues with Google Cloud:

- **Data Breach:** There are many ways data breaches or data loss can occur in Google Cloud. It can be an internal or an external issue, but mostly it is an internal error that paves the way for a data breach. Sometimes an employee can accidentally make file sharing public or email the files to an unauthorised person, etc. Hence, it is essential to ensure data loss prevention policies are appropriately set to prevent unauthorised access or loss of sensitive data.

- **Access Management:** With on-premises server hosting, system admins had complete control over data access management. But with cloud computing, poor encryption key management will lead to unauthorized access to sensitive data.

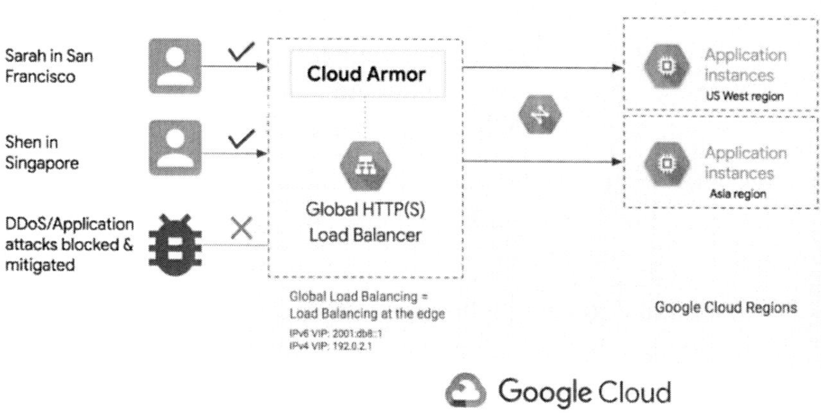

Fig 4.0 - Google Cloud Security

Malicious actors can pose as legitimate users to read, modify and delete your data. Hence, it is essential to create identity groups based on their privileges and rotate keys regularly. Also, unused accounts need to be deleted immediately.

- **Account Takeover:** Another major security challenge with Google Cloud is account takeover. Even though Google has introduced 2- step authentication and suspicious login identification, they are only helpful if these settings are enabled.
- **Misconfiguration of Cloud Resources:** One of the most common risks in GCP is misconfiguration of cloud services and resources. This can happen due to a lack of understanding of the platform's settings and features, leading to inadvertent exposure of data or services to the public internet.
- **Inadequate Access Controls:** Improper management of Identity and Access Management (IAM) policies can lead to excessive or inappropriate access rights, increasing the risk of data breaches or unauthorised actions.
- **Compromised Service Accounts:** Service accounts in GCP are used to grant permissions to services and applications. If these accounts are compromised, an attacker could gain extensive access to GCP resources.
- **Data Breaches:** Even with GCP's security measures, there is always a risk of data breaches, either through external attacks or internal vulnerabilities, such as unpatched systems or software flaws.
- **Insufficient Network Security:** Inadequate network security controls can expose GCP resources to potential network-based attacks, such as DDoS attacks or unauthorised network penetrations.
- **Insecure APIs:** GCP services are often accessed and managed through APIs. If these APIs are not properly secured, they can become a target for cyberattacks.
- **Compliance Risks:** Failing to adhere to regulatory compliance requirements in GCP environments can lead to legal and financial penalties. Compliance risks are especially pertinent for industries

subject to specific regulations, like healthcare or finance.

- **Vendor Lock-in Risks:** Dependence on GCP-specific technologies and services can lead to vendor lock-in, making it difficult and costly to migrate to another cloud provider in the future.

5. Building a Cloud Security Strategy

Developing a cloud security strategy involves a series of critical steps to ensure that your organisation's assets are comprehensively protected.

1) Defining Your Assets:

Scope: Begin by cataloguing both physical and digital assets. This includes hardware, software, network infrastructure, and especially the data stored and processed within these systems.

Sensitive Data Identification: Pay particular attention to sensitive data, such as personal information, intellectual property, financial records, and any other data critical to your organisation.

Asset Categorisation: Classify assets based on their criticality and sensitivity. This helps in prioritising security efforts.

2) Identifying Your Threats:

Threat Landscape Analysis: Understand the range of threats specific to cloud environments, such as data breaches, account hijacking, insecure APIs, and service traffic hijacking.

Source Identification: Identify potential sources of threats, including internal risks like malicious insiders or negligent employees, and external risks like hackers or third-party service providers.

Risk Assessment: Evaluate how likely each type of threat is, and the potential impact on your organisation.

3) Determining Your Controls:

Data Sensitivity Assessment: Assess the sensitivity of the data being stored in the cloud. The level of sensitivity will dictate the rigour of the controls needed.

Control Types: Consider a mix of preventive, detective, and corrective controls. This includes encryption, access controls, monitoring systems, and incident response mechanisms.

Cloud Service Models: Your security controls will also vary depending on whether you're using Infrastructure as a Service (IaaS), Platform as a Service (PaaS), or Software as a Service (SaaS).

4) Developing Policies and Procedures:

Policy Framework: Develop comprehensive policies covering aspects like user access, data encryption, incident response, and compliance with legal and regulatory standards.

Standard Operating Procedures (SOPs): Create detailed procedures for routine and emergency tasks, ensuring that employees know their roles and responsibilities in maintaining cloud security.

5) Regular Review and Update:

Continuous Monitoring: Regularly monitor and review the effectiveness of your security controls.

Adaptation to Changes: Update your security strategy in response to new threats, technological advancements, or changes in business operations.

6) Training and Awareness:

Employee Training: Conduct regular training sessions for employees to raise awareness about cloud security risks and best practices.

Culture of Security: Foster a workplace culture where security is a shared responsibility.

7) Compliance and Legal Considerations:

Regulatory Compliance: Ensure that your cloud security strategy aligns with industry regulations and standards.

Legal Implications: Understand the legal implications of storing data in the cloud, especially in different jurisdictions.

8) Vendor Management:

Cloud Service Provider Evaluation: Thoroughly assess potential cloud service providers for their security measures and compliance standards.

Service Level Agreements (SLAs): Ensure SLAs with cloud providers include security requirements and responsibilities.

By following these expanded steps, organisations can establish a robust cloud security strategy that not only protects their assets but also aligns with their overall business objectives and regulatory requirements.

3. Best Practices in Monitoring Cloud Security

To overcome any security risks, the following best practices must be followed to prevent unauthorised access, data loss, and other security issues. For convenience, we've separated the best practices for every cloud provider below:

Implementing best practices in Amazon AWS is crucial for maintaining a secure and efficient cloud environment.

Amazon Web Services (AWS):

1. **Enable CloudTrail for Anomaly Detection:** AWS CloudTrail provides a record of actions taken in your AWS account. Analysing these logs helps detect unusual activity.

- **Best Practices:**
  - **Continuous Monitoring**: Set up continuous monitoring of CloudTrail logs.
  - **Integration with Monitoring Tools**: Integrate CloudTrail with AWS CloudWatch or third-party SIEM solutions for comprehensive analysis.
  - **Alerts**: Configure alerts for unexpected API calls or unauthorised resource changes.

9) **Use EBS Encryption: Encrypting Amazon Elastic Block Store (EBS) volumes protects data at rest.**

- **Best Practices:**
  - **Default Encryption:** Set new EBS volumes to be encrypted by default.
  - **Key Management**: Use AWS Key Management Service (KMS) to manage encryption keys securely.

❖ **Encrypt Existing Volumes**: Encrypt existing unencrypted EBS volumes.

10) **Implement Identity and Access Management (IAM): IAM manages access to AWS services and resources securely.**

- **Best Practices:**

    ❖ **Least Privilege:** Grant minimum necessary permissions.

    ❖ **Multi-Factor Authentication (MFA)**: Enforce MFA for added security.

    ❖ **Regular Audits**: Review and audit IAM permissions and roles regularly.

    ❖ **IAM Policies**: Define permissions programmatically using IAM policies.

11) **Ensure AWS Policies are Up to Date: Keeping AWS policies current ensures compliance and security.**

- **Best Practices:**

    ❖ **Regular Review**: Periodically review security policies for relevancy and compliance.

    ❖ **Automate Compliance Checking:** Use AWS Config to automate compliance checks.

    ❖ **Update with AWS Best Practices:** Incorporate AWS's latest best practice recommendations.

Additional Best Practices:

1. **Secure Network Configurations:** Utilise Virtual Private Cloud (VPC), Security Groups, and Network Access Control Lists (NACLs) to control network access.

2. **Regular Security Audits:** Use AWS Trusted Advisor for analysis and conduct regular penetration tests.

3. **Backup and Disaster Recovery:** Use automated backups with services like Amazon RDS and EBS snapshots. Develop and test a disaster recovery plan.

By implementing these best practices, you can enhance the security and compliance of your AWS environment effectively.

Best Practices for Azure

Adopting best practices in Microsoft Azure is key to maximising cloud security and efficiency. Here's an expanded look at the practices you've outlined:

1) **Use Privileged Access Workstations (PAWs) for Enhanced Security:**
   - **Purpose:** PAWs provide a dedicated environment for sensitive tasks protected from internet attacks.
   - **Best Practices:**
   - ❖ **Physical and Logical Isolation**: Keep PAWs separate from daily-use workstations to prevent exposure to attacks.
   - ❖ **Restrict Internet Access**: Limit internet access to reduce exposure to malicious content.
   - ❖ **Secure Configuration**: Ensure PAWs are configured with high-security standards and updated regularly.
2) **Limit Network, User, and Administrator Access:**
   - **Purpose:** Minimise access to reduce the attack surface and potential for breaches.
   - **Best Practices:**
   - ❖ **Least Privilege Principle**: Grant users and administrators only necessary access.
   - ❖ **Network Segmentation**: Use AWS Virtual Private Cloud (VPC) to segment network resources.
   - ❖ **Identity and Access Management (IAM):** Implement IAM policies to control access to AWS resources.

3) **Encrypt Virtual Disks and Disk Storage:**

- **Purpose:** Encryption protects data at rest from unauthorised access.

- **Best Practices:**

- ❖ **AWS Key Management Service (KMS)**: Use KMS to manage encryption keys.

- ❖ **Amazon Elastic Block Store (EBS)**: Encrypt EBS volumes to protect data stored in them.

4) **Utilise AWS Key Management Service (KMS) for Key Management:**

- **Purpose:** KMS safeguards cryptographic keys used by cloud applications.

- **Best Practices:**

- ❖ **Centralised Key Management**: Manage keys centrally with KMS.

- ❖ **Access Controls:** Configure IAM policies to control access to KMS.

5) **Continuous Monitoring with AWS Security Hub:**

- **Purpose:** AWS Security Hub provides unified security management and threat protection.

- **Best Practices:**

- ❖ **Enable Security Hub**: Activate Security Hub to gain insights into security posture.

- ❖ **Automated Compliance Checks**: Use automated compliance checks to maintain security standards.

6) **Use Privileged Access Workstations (PAWs) for Enhanced Security:**

- **Purpose:** PAWs provide a secure environment for sensitive tasks.

- **Best Practices:**

- ❖ **Physical and Logical Isolation**: Keep PAWs separate from daily-use workstations.

- ❖ **Restrict Internet Access:** Limit internet access to PAWs.
- ❖ **Secure Configuration:** Ensure PAWs are configured securely.

7) **Limit Network, User, and Administrator Access:**
   - **Purpose:** Minimise access to reduce the attack surface.
   - **Best Practices:**
   - ❖ **Least Privilege Principle**: Grant minimal access required.
   - ❖ **Network Segmentation**: Use Azure Virtual Networks for network segmentation.
   - ❖ **Role-Based Access Control (RBAC)**: Implement RBAC to manage access.

8) **Encrypt Virtual Disks and Disk Storage:**
   - **Purpose:** Encryption protects data at rest.
   - **Best Practices:**
   - ❖ **Azure Disk Encryption**: Encrypt virtual machine disks using Azure Disk Encryption.
   - ❖ **Key Management**: Manage encryption keys securely with Azure Key Vault.

9) **Utilise Azure Key Vault for Key Management:**
   - **Purpose:** Safeguard cryptographic keys and secrets.
   - **Best Practices:**
   - ❖ **Centralised Key Management:** Manage keys centrally with Azure Key Vault.
   - ❖ **Access Policies:** Configure access policies to control access to Key Vault.

10) **Continuous Monitoring with Azure Security Centre:**

- **Purpose:** Provides unified security management and advanced threat protection.
- **Best Practices:**

❖ **Enable Security Centre:** Utilise Azure Security Centre across all subscriptions.

❖ **Automated Security Assessment**: Take advantage of an automated security assessment.

❖ **Custom Alerts and Policies**: Set up custom alerts and policies as per requirements.

Additional Best Practices for Azure:

1) **Implement Azure Application Gateway for Web Application Firewall (WAF):**

- **Purpose:** Protect web applications from common attacks.
- **Best Practices:**

❖ **Enable WAF**: Use Azure Application Gateway with WAF to protect web applications.

❖ **Custom Rules**: Create custom WAF rules tailored to application requirements.

2) **Regular Backup and Disaster Recovery Planning:**

- **Purpose:** Ensures business continuity and data protection.
- Best Practices:

❖ **Azure Backup**: Use Azure Backup for data backup.

❖ **Azure Site Recovery:** Implement Azure Site Recovery for disaster recovery.

By implementing these best practices, you can significantly enhance the security and resilience of your Azure cloud environment, ensuring that your resources are both protected and compliant with organisational standards and industry best practices.

3) Google Cloud Platform:

Implementing best practices in Google Cloud Platform (GCP) is essential for securing and optimising your cloud environment.

4) Utilise GCP IAM for Access Control:

Google Cloud Identity & Access Management (IAM) allows you to manage who has access to your GCP resources and what they can do with those resources. Following the principle of least privilege, grant only the necessary permissions to IAM users and service accounts. Use Role-Based Access Control (RBAC) by assigning predefined or custom roles based on job functions. Regularly review IAM audit logs to monitor access and changes to permissions, ensuring that your GCP environment remains secure and well-regulated.

5) Effective Use of Groups and Service Accounts:

Groups and service accounts simplify user and permission management in GCP. Organise users into groups based on their roles and assign permissions to groups rather than individual users. This practice streamlines permission management and reduces complexity. Use service accounts for server-to-server interactions, adhering to the principle of least privilege to ensure that applications have only the necessary permissions. This approach enhances security and simplifies identity management within your cloud environment.

6) Define Your Resource Hierarchy:

A well-planned resource hierarchy helps in organising and managing GCP resources efficiently. Set up an organisation node as the root node in the hierarchy, and organize resources into projects, which serve as containers for your GCP resources. Use folders to group projects under the organisation node for better governance and structure. This organised approach makes it easier to manage permissions, billing, and policies across your GCP environment, providing a clear structure for your cloud resources.

7) Set Firewall Rules to Manage Traffic:

Firewall rules in GCP control the traffic to and from instances in your Virtual Private Cloud (VPC). Implement a default deny rule for inbound traffic, and allow only specific traffic as needed to minimise exposure to threats. Use firewall rules to segment network traffic and enforce network boundaries, enhancing security. Enable logging for firewall rules to monitor and audit network traffic, ensuring that any suspicious activity is detected and addressed promptly.

8) Use VPCs and Subnets for Network Mapping:

Virtual Private Clouds (VPCs) and subnets enable you to build a logically isolated network within Google Cloud. Create custom VPCs rather than using the default VPC to have more control over network settings. Design subnets carefully, considering IP address ranges and regional availability for better network management and security. For enhanced security, use private IP addresses and private Google access where possible, ensuring that your network architecture supports secure and efficient operations.

Additional Best Practices:

1) Regular Data Backups and Disaster Recovery Planning:

Regularly back up data using Google Cloud Storage and Persistent Disks. Ensure data redundancy across multiple geographic locations to protect against data loss and enable swift recovery in the event of a disaster. A robust disaster recovery plan ensures business continuity and data integrity.

2) Encrypt Data at Rest and in Transit:

GCP automatically encrypts data at rest and in transit, but consider additional encryption layers for sensitive data. Utilise Google Cloud Key Management Service (KMS) for managing cryptographic keys. This ensures that your data remains secure and protected from unauthorised access, both during transmission and while stored.

3) Implement Monitoring and Logging:

Use Google Cloud's Stackdriver for logging, monitoring, and diagnostics. Stack driver provides insights into the health, performance, and availability of cloud applications and services. By implementing comprehensive monitoring and logging, you can detect issues early, optimise performance, and maintain a secure and reliable cloud environment.

By adopting these best practices, you can significantly improve the security, efficiency, and manageability of your Google Cloud Platform environment, ensuring a robust and compliant cloud infrastructure.

A. Analysing Real-World Scenarios

Case Study: Online Payment Platform Breach

Scenario: In 2020, a leading online payment platform experienced a significant data breach. Attackers exploited a vulnerability in the application's API, leading to the exposure of millions of user records. This platform, widely used for its convenience and reach, found itself in the headlines as customers' sensitive financial data, including names, email addresses, and partial credit card information, was compromised.

Analysis: The breach was primarily due to insufficient API security measures. A key vulnerability was inadequate rate limiting, which allowed attackers to perform automated attacks, often referred to as "credential stuffing" or brute force attacks. Moreover, the API lacked robust authentication mechanisms. The platform relied on basic API keys and tokens without implementing more secure, dynamic authentication methods. This oversight made it easier for attackers to gain unauthorised access.

Industry reports highlighted that the platform did not employ proper logging and monitoring of API calls, which could have detected the anomalous behaviour sooner. The absence of these security layers provided attackers a larger window to exploit the system and extract data.

Key Takeaway: This breach underscores the critical need for comprehensive API security. Here are some key lessons and best practices drawn from this incident:

1. **Rate Limiting:** Implement strict rate limiting to prevent automated attacks. Limiting the number of API requests that can be made in a given timeframe can help mitigate the risk of brute force and credential stuffing attacks.
2. **Robust Authentication Mechanisms:** Use multi-factor authentication (MFA) for API access. This could include OAuth, API tokens with expiration, and ensuring that tokens are tied to specific IP addresses or usage patterns.

3. **Regular Vulnerability Assessments:** Conduct frequent security audits and vulnerability assessments of APIs. Penetration testing can help identify weaknesses before attackers can exploit them.

4. **Dynamic Monitoring and Logging:** Implement continuous monitoring and logging of API calls to detect and respond to unusual patterns of activity. Real-time alerts for suspicious activities can significantly reduce the time to detect and mitigate breaches.

5. **Data Encryption:** Ensure that all sensitive data is encrypted both at rest and in transit. This adds layer of security, making it more difficult for attackers to extract useful information even if they gain access.

In 2021, the cost of a data breach in the financial sector was reported to average $5.72 million per incident, according to IBM's Cost of a Data Breach Report. This includes both direct costs, such as legal fees and technical recovery efforts, and indirect costs, like reputational damage and customer loss. The affected payment platform saw a 20% drop in user trust and a significant number of users migrating to competitors within months of the breach.

This case highlights that as online payment platforms continue to evolve, they must prioritise security measures, particularly around their APIs, to protect user data and maintain trust.

B. Effective Security Strategies in Action for Startups

Case Study: Secure Mobile Payment App Launch

Start-up Scenario: A fintech start-up, Pay Secure, developed a mobile payment app with a strong emphasis on security right from the beginning. Understanding the sensitive nature of financial transactions and the potential for cyber threats, the start-up aimed to create a secure and trustworthy platform for users.

Strategy: Pay Secure implemented a multi-layered security strategy to protect user data and transactions:

1. **End-to-End Encryption:** All data transmitted between the user's device and Pay Secure servers was encrypted using advanced encryption standards (AES-256). This ensured that even if data was intercepted, it would be unreadable to unauthorised parties.

2. **Biometric Authentication:** To enhance user authentication, Pay Secure integrated biometric authentication methods, such as fingerprint scanning and facial recognition, leveraging the security features available on modern smartphones. This added an extra layer of security beyond traditional passwords.

3. **Real-Time Transaction Monitoring:** Pay Secure deployed real-time transaction monitoring systems powered by machine learning algorithms. These systems continuously analysed transaction patterns and flagged any suspicious activities for immediate review. This proactive approach helped in detecting and preventing fraudulent transactions before they could cause harm.

Outcome: Despite being a new entrant in the competitive mobile payment market, Pay Secure quickly gained consumer trust due to its robust security measures. Some key outcomes included:

1. **User Adoption and Growth:** Within the first year of launch, Pay Secure saw a rapid increase in user adoption, growing its user base by 150%. The app was downloaded over 500,000 times, with a high retention rate of 85% after three months.

2. **Positive Customer Feedback:** Users praised the app's security features, particularly the ease and reliability of biometric authentication. Surveys indicated that 95% of users felt more secure using Pay Secure compared to other payment apps.

3. **Market Recognition:** Pay Secure's strong security focus was recognised by industry experts. The start-up received the "Best Mobile Security Solution" award at the 2023 Fintech Innovation Conference. Additionally, Pay Secure's approach to security was highlighted in several tech publications, further enhancing its reputation.

4. **Low Fraud Incidence:** Thanks to the real-time transaction monitoring system, Pay Secure experienced significantly lower fraud incidence rates compared to industry averages. While the average fraud rate in mobile payments was around 1.5%, Pay Secure maintained a fraud rate of just 0.2%, showcasing the effectiveness of its security measures.

This case study illustrates how prioritising security from the outset can be a significant market differentiator for fintech start-ups. By implementing advanced security features and continuously monitoring for threats, Pay Secure not only protected its users but also built a strong foundation of trust and credibility in the competitive mobile payment market.

Additional Considerations for Fintech Companies

- **Compliance and Regulations**: Fintech companies must adhere to various financial regulations and standards like PCI DSS, GDPR, and others, depending on their operating regions.
- **Cloud Security**: As fintech often relies on cloud services, they must ensure cloud configurations are secure, practice strict access controls, and employ encryption both in transit and at rest.
- **Emerging Technology Risks**: Fintech companies are at the forefront of adopting new technologies like blockchain and AI. Understanding and mitigating the risks associated with these technologies is essential.

Final Thoughts

With the growing reliance on cloud computing, security challenges have also increased. With on-premises hosting, data is always under control by the system admin.

But with the advent of cloud computing and data being moved to the cloud and accessed by many devices, security and compliance have become very complex.

While cloud providers offer various security measures, including application security and infrastructure, the cloud security architecture is often considered a shared responsibility model.

Chapter - 4

Cybersecurity Investments: Strategizing fOr Optimal PrOtectiOn andEfficiency

"Every breach of security begins with a silent compromise of our trust."

— Timsux Wales

In today's digital age, where technology rapidly evolves, and cyber threats become increasingly sophisticated, startups must prioritize cybersecurity. The initial stage of a startup is critical; it's a time when they establish their market presence and build customer trust. Investing in cybersecurity is not merely a protective measure but a strategic investment that safeguards the startup's intellectual property, customer data, and overall reputation.

For startups, a security breach can have devastating consequences, including financial losses, legal liabilities, and, most critically, irreparable damage to customer trust and brand image. Therefore, recognising the importance of cybersecurity and allocating appropriate financial resources is essential for a startup's long-term success and sustainability.

Startups often operate with limited resources and need help allocating their budget to meet various business needs. However, underestimating the importance of cybersecurity can be a grave mistake. The cost of implementing robust cybersecurity measures is significantly lower than the expenses associated with a data breach, which include regulatory fines, legal fees, and loss of business.

Investing in cybersecurity also aligns with building a resilient business foundation, as it prepares the startup to handle cyber threats proactively. This investment goes beyond deploying firewalls or antivirus software; it encompasses a comprehensive approach involving risk management, employee training, secure coding practices, regular security audits, and adopting industry best practices.

Moreover, for startups, especially in the technology and fintech sectors, demonstrating a solid commitment to cybersecurity can be a crucial differentiator in the market. Investors and customers are increasingly aware of cyber risks and often make decisions based on a company's security posture. A robust cybersecurity strategy can thus become a competitive advantage, attracting investment and building customer loyalty.

It's also essential for startups to understand that cybersecurity is a continuous process requiring ongoing investment and adaptation to evolving threats. In essence, the financial investment in cybersecurity is not just a cost—it's a critical component of a startup's value proposition and a driver of long-term growth and success.

Objectives

After studying this chapter, you will understand:

- Understanding the Importance of Financial Investment in Cybersecurity for Startups
- Understand the Key Considerations in Creating a Cybersecurity Budget
- The cost-effective security strategies
- The Right Balance Between Investing in Security and Maintaining Overall Financial Health
- Case Studies on Budgeting for Security in Startup Environments

Budgeting Basics for Cybersecurity

Key Considerations in Creating a Cybersecurity Budget

- **Creating the Budget**

The first step when creating a cybersecurity budget is conducting a thorough risk assessment to identify the organisation's security needs. This involves understanding the types of data held, the potential threats, and the regulatory requirements the company must adhere to. Budgeting must account for preventive measures (like firewalls, encryption, and antivirus software) and reactive measures (such as incident response tools and disaster recovery plans). It's essential to prioritise spending on areas with the highest risk while considering the overall impact on business operations. This budget should be flexible enough to adapt to emerging threats and include funds for regular employee training and awareness programs.

- **Gaining Sponsorship from Board and Management**

To secure the necessary sponsorship and backing from the board and management for effective cybersecurity budgeting, it's critical to articulate the significance of cybersecurity in terms that resonate with business leaders. This often means framing the conversation around risk management and business continuity, steering clear of overly technical jargon. Crucially, aligning the cybersecurity strategy with the organisation's wider business objectives is key. This approach demonstrates how investments in cybersecurity are not just protective measures but are, in fact, instrumental in supporting the overall goals and growth of the business.

Presenting a Case Study of a Recent Cyber Incident

Case Study: The SolarWinds Cyberattack

Background:

The SolarWinds cyberattack, discovered in late 2020, is one of the most sophisticated and significant cyber espionage efforts in recent history. This incident involved the compromise of the Orion software platform by SolarWinds, which produces software for managing and monitoring computer networks.

How the Attack Happened:

The attackers, believed to be state-sponsored, managed to insert a vulnerability into the software updates of the Orion platform. This malicious code, once executed, opened backdoors into the networks of SolarWinds' clients. The breach was not just a single event but a series of complex operations that remained undetected for months. It affected numerous high-profile targets, including US government agencies and major corporations.

Consequences:

The SolarWinds attack had far-reaching implications. It exposed sensitive data, including national security information and intellectual property. The scale and sophistication of the attack led to a reevaluation of network security practices, especially concerning supply chain and third-party software vulnerabilities.

Lessons Learned:

1. **Supply Chain Vulnerability**: The attack highlighted the need for enhanced security measures in supply chains and the importance of vetting third-party vendors and software.
2. **Continuous Monitoring and Detection**: It underscored the significance of continuous network monitoring and the implementation of advanced detection mechanisms to identify suspicious activities.
3. **Patch Management**: The necessity for timely and efficient patch management strategies became evident, as delays in updating software can open windows of opportunity for attackers.
4. **Incident Response Plan**: A robust incident response plan is crucial. Organisations affected by the SolarWinds breach had to mobilise quickly to assess the impact and mitigate further risks.
5. Focus on Cyber Resilience beyond prevention, organisations must focus on building cyber resilience, ensuring they can maintain critical functions and quickly recover in the event of a breach.

Impact on Cybersecurity Budgeting:

This case study is a crucial example for businesses considering their cybersecurity budgets. It demonstrates that cybersecurity is not just an IT issue but a strategic business concern. Investments in comprehensive security measures, including advanced threat detection systems, robust vendor risk management, and employee training programs, are vital. The SolarWinds incident proves that the cost of preventing a breach is significantly less than the financial and reputational costs of dealing with the aftermath of a cyberattack.

Cost-Effective Security Strategies

Strategies for Maximizing Cybersecurity Effectiveness While Minimizing Costs

1) **Prioritising Based on Risk Assessment:**
    - **Key Approach**: Conduct a thorough risk assessment to identify and prioritise the most significant threats and vulnerabilities.

Focus resources on areas that would cause the most damage to the business if compromised.

- **Benefits**: This approach ensures that limited resources are not wasted on low-impact risks, thereby maximising the cost- cost-effectiveness of security investments.

2) **Leveraging Open Source and Free Security Tools:**
   - **Utilisation of Available Tools**: Numerous open-source and free security tools can provide robust security features comparable to paid versions.
   - **Considerations**: Ensure that these tools are reputable and regularly updated. They should be carefully evaluated and tested to meet the organisation's security needs

3) **Employee Training and Awareness Programs:**
   - **Importance**: Human error is often a significant vulnerability. Regular training for employees on basic cybersecurity practices can significantly reduce risks.
   - **Cost-Effectiveness**: This is a relatively low-cost approach to prevent a wide range of security incidents, from phishing attacks to accidental data breaches.

4) **Implementing Strong Policies and Procedures:**
   - **Development of Policies**: Develop and enforce robust security policies and procedures. This includes password policies, BYOD (Bring Your Own Device) policies, and data handling procedures.

- **Impact**: Strong policies can often mitigate risks without expensive technological solutions.

5) **Regular Audits and Continuous Monitoring:**
   - **Routine Checkups**: Conduct regular security audits and continuous monitoring of networks and systems to quickly identify and address vulnerabilities.
   - **Cost Saving**: Early detection of security issues can prevent costly breaches and data loss incidents.

6) **Outsourcing to Managed Security Service Providers (MSSPs):**
   - **Strategic Outsourcing**: For some businesses, outsourcing cybersecurity to MSSPs can be more cost-effective than developing an in-house team.
   - **Benefits**: MSSPs provide expertise and 24/7 monitoring services, often cheaper than maintaining a dedicated internal team.

7) **Utilising Cloud-Based Security Solutions:**
   - **Cloud Advantages**: Cloud-based security solutions can be more affordable due to their scalability and lack of physical infrastructure requirements.
   - **Flexibility**: These solutions often offer pay-as-you-go models, allowing businesses to pay only for what they use.

Throughout various strategies, a particularly effective method I've observed is adopting a supply and demand mindset. While not always applied in a literal sense, this perspective steers you towards a more business-oriented approach when requesting resources. Consequently, this tactic enhances your likelihood of obtaining the necessary assets, as it positions you as a responsible steward of resources in the eyes of other executives. Achieving this status is advantageous, as it cultivates a reputation for maximising every dollar or personnel resource allocated to you, significantly contributing to the organisation's financial success or mission objectives.

Consider approaching security budgeting through the lens of supply and demand. By managing both aspects, you transform the budgeting process into a risk management exercise. Even if this methodology isn't formally outlined, it inherently brings a clearer thought process. Moreover, it demonstrates to your business that you're adopting a commercial mindset, focusing on how to effectively curb the continuous escalation of the security budget.

Cybersecurity Tools and Practices

Organisations can achieve a strong cybersecurity posture by adopting these cost-effective security strategies without incurring excessive costs. ManageEngine's security information and event management (SIEM) solutions empower startups to strengthen threat detection, accelerate incident response, ensure regulatory compliance, and minimise security risks.

- **UEBA:** Analyse logs from different sources leveraging machine learning and AI-driven behaviour analytics to identify abnormal user, host, and entity activities and offer insights through risk scores, trends, and reports.
- **Real-time security analytics:** Collect and analyse logs from various sources, including end-user devices, and gain contextual insights to conduct hassle-free investigations, enabling faster threat resolution.
- **Integrated CASB:** Regulate access to sensitive data in the cloud, track the use of sanctioned and unsanctioned applications, and detect the use of shadow IT applications.
- **Threat investigation workbench:** Analyse flagged threats, check IP and URL reputation, and take action from the SIEM console to investigate entities with additional data.
- **SOAR:** Expedite incident resolution by prioritising security threats and automating responses to detected security incidents through standard workflows.
- **Integrated compliance management:** Ensure compliance with PCI DSS, GDPR, FISMA, HIPAA, SOX, GLBA, and more using pre-built and custom reports.

Key product: Log360

Visit **www.manageengine.com/siem to know more.**

It's about being wise with resources, understanding the threat landscape, and leveraging the right tools and practices to protect against the most pressing risks.

Open-source tools can also be explored in cybersecurity, offering cost-effective and often highly customizable solutions for various security needs.

Here's a breakdown of open-source tools across different cybersecurity categories:

1) **Security Information and Event Management (SIEM)**
   - **Elasticsearch, Logstash, and Kibana (ELK Stack)**: Often used together for powerful SIEM capabilities. Elasticsearch provides search and data indexing, Logstash handles data processing and ingestion, and Kibana offers data visualisation.
   - **Ossec**: An open-source, host-based intrusion detection system that performs log analysis, file integrity checking, policy monitoring, rootkit detection, and real-time alerting.

2) **Cloud Security**
   - **Clair**: An open-source project for the static analysis of vulnerabilities in application containers (like Docker).
   - **Cloud Custodian**: Offers automated cloud security, governance, and management. It's a rules engine for managing public cloud accounts and resources.

3) **Code Scanning (Static Application Security Testing - SAST)**
   - **SonarQube**: Provides continuous inspection of code quality to detect bugs, code smells, and security vulnerabilities.
   - **Brakeman**: A static analysis tool for Ruby on Rails applications, focusing on security issues.

4) **Container Scanning**

- **Anchor-Engine**: Analyses Docker images, checks for vulnerabilities, and applies custom policies.
- **Trivia**: A simple and comprehensive vulnerability scanner for containers, suitable for CI.

5) **Antivirus**

- **ClamAV**: An open-source antivirus engine detecting trojans, viruses, malware, and other malicious threats.
- **Sophos Antivirus for Linux**: Provides detection and disinfection capabilities for Linux systems.

6) **Firewall**

- **pfSense**: A firewall and router that also features VPN, intrusion detection/prevention, and other capabilities.
- **OPNsense**: A user-friendly firewall and routing platform, including features like traffic shaping, load balancing, and virtual private networking.

7) **Web Application Firewall (WAF)**

- **ModSecurity**: It is often used with the Apache HTTP Server and provides various security features for web applications.
- **NAXSI**: A high-performance, low-rules maintenance WAF for Nginx, focusing on a positive security model.

Each of these tools offers unique features and capabilities, and the choice of instrument can depend on an organisation's specific requirements and environment. Open-source tools require careful setup and management but provide a flexible and often powerful alternative to commercial security solutions.

Open-source tools for vulnerability scanning

Open-source tools for vulnerability scanning are widely used in cybersecurity for identifying potential security weaknesses in systems and networks. Here are some notable tools in this category:

1) **OpenVAS (Open Vulnerability Assessment System):**

- **Description**: A full-featured vulnerability scanner. Its capabilities include unauthenticated testing, authenticated testing, various high and low-level internet and industrial protocols, performance tuning for large-scale scans, and a powerful internal programming language to implement any vulnerability test.
- **Use Case**: Ideal for comprehensive vulnerability assessments across various network devices and platforms.

2) **Nmap (Network Mapper):**
   - **Description**: Primarily used for network discovery and security auditing. Nmap uses raw IP packets to determine available network hosts, their services and operating systems, and types of packet filters/firewalls.
   - **Use Case**: Best suited for network inventory, managing service upgrade schedules, and monitoring host or service uptime.

3) **Nikto:**
   - **Description**: An open-source web server scanner that checks for dangerous files/CGIs, outdated server software, and other problems. It performs generic and server-type-specific checks.
   - **Use Case**: Effective for scanning web servers for potentially harmful files and server misconfigurations.

4) **SQL map:**
   - **Description**: An open-source penetration testing tool that automates detecting and exploiting SQL injection flaws and taking over database servers.
   - **Use Case**: Instrumental in testing web applications for SQL injection vulnerabilities.

5) **w3af (Web Application Attack and Audit Framework):**
   - **Description**: A web application security scanner that identifies and exploits vulnerabilities.
   - **Use Case**: Good for auditing web application security, especially for custom-built applications.

6) **OWASP ZAP (Zed Attack Proxy):**

- **Description**: One of the world's most popular free security tools, ZAP, is used for finding vulnerabilities in web applications.
- **Use Case**: Excellent for beginners and experienced testers, helpful in CI/CD pipelines.

7) **Metasploit Framework:**

- **Description**: A tool for developing and executing exploit code against a remote target machine. It also includes means for network reconnaissance and vulnerability scanning.
- **Use Case**: Best suited for penetration testing and developing new security tools.

8) **Arachni:**

- **Description**: A feature-full, modular, high-performance Ruby framework aimed towards helping penetration testers and administrators evaluate the security of web applications.
- **Use Case**: Ideal for web application scanning, focusing on comprehensiveness and performance.

Each of these tools has its strengths and is best suited for different aspects of vulnerability scanning. Their open-source nature allows for customisation and flexibility, making them valuable resources for organisations looking to enhance their security posture without incurring significant costs.

Balancing Security and Financial Stability

Finding the Right Balance Between Investing in Security and Maintaining Overall Financial Health

Imagine you're walking a tightrope between two skyscrapers. A giant piggy bank labelled "Financial Stability" gently swayed in the breeze on one side. On the other side, an equally big, somewhat menacing-looking padlock marked "Cybersecurity." Your job is to get across without dropping your budgetary briefcase or getting knocked off by a sudden gust of wind called "Unforeseen Expenses." Welcome to the thrilling world of balancing cybersecurity investments with financial prudence!

In this high-stakes balancing act, the key is not to lean too much toward the piggy bank, tempting as it may be, lest you leave your digital doors open to cyber bandits. Nor should you edge too close to the padlock, as you might end up locking yourself out of your bank account due to overspending on security.

The first step in this balance is clearly understanding your company's security needs. It's like knowing the length of your tightrope – you wouldn't want to find out halfway across that you needed more rope! Conduct a thorough risk assessment to identify your vulnerabilities and focus your spending there. This ensures you're not splurging on a state- of-the-art security system for a digital lemonade stand.

Next, consider the potential cost of a security breach – it's not just about the immediate financial loss but also the long-term damage to your business reputation. Think of it as an unexpected gust of wind; without a proper safety net (read: effective security measures), you risk a fall that could be difficult to recover from. Investing in cybersecurity is akin to wearing a safety harness; it might feel like an unnecessary constraint when the weather's fine, but you'll be thankful for it when things get windy.

Finally, remember the value of employee training. It's often the most cost-effective defence against many common cyber threats. Educate your team about the importance of strong passwords – no, "password123" doesn't count – and the dangers of phishing emails. Think of it as giving everyone on your team their tightrope-walking poles to help maintain balance.

Balancing cybersecurity investments with financial health requires a blend of strategic planning, understanding of risks, and acrobatic skills. Like a skilled tightrope walker, you must maintain focus, assess your environment, and take calculated steps. And remember, sometimes the most significant risk is taking no risk at all – especially if that leaves your digital windows open for anyone to climb through!

Demonstrating Return on Investment

Articulating the return on investment (ROI) of cybersecurity spending can be challenging, but it is crucial for sustained financial commitment. ROI can be demonstrated through the potential cost savings from averting data breaches, including avoiding fines, legal fees, and reputational damage.

Metrics such as reduced incident response times, lower rates of malware infection, and employee competency levels in cybersecurity practices can also illustrate ROI. Additionally, emphasise the value of cybersecurity in enabling business initiatives, such as digital transformation or entry into new markets, which may be hindered.

In today's digital landscape, marked by an omnipresence of platforms, both on-premises and cloud-based, adopting a universal standard of security controls is imperative. This standard should encompass a range of measures, from patching and vulnerability management to identity and access management, network segmentation, and robust software security. The goal should be to continually enhance this baseline, both in terms of the breadth of features and controls and the depth of assurance and rigour they provide. However, it's crucial to acknowledge the reality of limited budgets. Elevating the baseline of security controls doesn't necessarily equate to escalating expenditure. Instead, the focus should be on decreasing the per-unit cost of implementing these controls, thereby allowing for widespread application across the network. It's not merely the initial cost of implementation that matters; more critical is the ongoing operational cost and its impact on productivity and user experience. To effectively raise the security standard, we must focus on reducing the costs associated with these controls, a task that demands both careful planning and persistent effort.

Planning and Managing Cybersecurity Spend

Having a strategic plan for cybersecurity spending is imperative. This plan should be regularly reviewed and updated to reflect the changing threat landscape and the organisation's growth. It's essential to allocate a portion of the budget for innovative security solutions to address emerging threats. Regularly reviewing and auditing the effectiveness of implemented security measures ensures that funds are used efficiently. Establishing partnerships with vendors and exploring different pricing models, such as subscriptions or pay-as-you-go, is also beneficial in minimising costs. Lastly, consider investing in cybersecurity insurance as a part of the cybersecurity budget to mitigate financial risks associated with potential cyber incidents.

A Structured Approach to Cybersecurity Investment

Strategising and planning the Return on Investment (ROI) in cybersecurity investment is critical for any organisation. It involves understanding the financial benefits of cybersecurity measures relative to their costs. Here's a structured approach:

1) **Identifying and Assessing Risks**
   - **Risk Assessment**: Start by identifying the cybersecurity risks that your organisation faces. Assess the potential impact and likelihood of these risks.
   - **Cost of Breaches**: Quantify the potential costs of data breaches, including direct costs (like fines and recovery expenses) and indirect costs (such as reputational damage and loss of customer trust).

2) **Aligning Security Investment with Business Objectives**
   - **Business Priorities**: Align cybersecurity strategies with business objectives. Understand how security investments support the overall goals and values of the organisation.
   - **Cost-Benefit Analysis**: Evaluate the cost of implementing specific cybersecurity measures against the benefit they provide in reducing risk.

3) **Measuring Direct and Indirect Benefits**
   - **Direct Benefits**: Include factors like reduced incidence of security breaches, lower costs related to breach mitigation, and compliance with regulatory standards.
   - **Indirect Benefits**: Consider the value of customer trust, market reputation, and competitive advantage gained through robust cybersecurity practices.

4) **Calculating ROI**
   - ROI Formula: Use a standard ROI formula: \(\text{ROI}= \frac{\text{Net Benefit of Investment (Benefit - Cost)}}{\text{Cost of Investment}} \times 100 \).
   - **Include All Costs**: Ensure that all costs of the cybersecurity

investment are included – this includes hardware, software, training, and workforce expenses.

- **Long-term Perspective**: Consider the long-term benefits and savings, such as avoidance of future breaches and sustained customer loyalty.

5) **Regular Review and Adjustment**
    - **Ongoing Evaluation**: Continuously monitor and review the effectiveness of cybersecurity measures.
    - **Adjust Strategy**: Be prepared to adjust your cybersecurity strategy and investments as new threats emerge and technologies evolve.

6) **Demonstrating ROI to Stakeholders**
    - **Communicate Effectively**: Present the calculated ROI to stakeholders clearly and concisely. Highlight how cybersecurity investments are protecting critical assets and supporting business growth.
    - **Use Metrics**: Use tangible metrics and real-world examples to demonstrate the effectiveness of cybersecurity investments.

7) **Leveraging Cybersecurity as a Business Enabler**
    - **Competitive Advantage**: Position robust cybersecurity as a value proposition to customers, especially in industries where data security is a critical concern.
    - **Support Business Initiatives**: Show how cybersecurity investments enable new business initiatives, such as digital transformation or expansion into new markets.

Case Studies on Budgeting for Security in Startup Environments

Case Study 1: Tech Startup Enhances Security Posture Within a Limited Budget

Background:

A growing tech startup specialising in cloud-based solutions faced challenges securing its expanding digital infrastructure. With limited financial resources, the company must prioritise its cybersecurity investments effectively.

Strategy:

- **Risk-Based Budgeting:** Conducted a comprehensive risk assessment to identify critical assets and vulnerabilities.
- **Cost-Effective Tools**: Implemented open-source and commercial cybersecurity tools to balance cost and effectiveness.
- **Employee Training:** Invested in employee cybersecurity training, recognising that human error can be a significant vulnerability.

Outcome:

- The startup successfully strengthened its security posture without overspending.
- Improved employee awareness led to a decrease in phishing attempts and other user-related breaches.
- The balanced approach to tool selection provided robust security without straining the budget.

Case Study 2: Fintech Startup Balances Compliance and Security Needs

Background:

A fintech startup operating in a heavily regulated industry requires a robust cybersecurity framework to protect sensitive financial data and comply with GDPR and PCI DSS regulations.

Strategy:

- **Compliance-Centric Budgeting**: Allocated budget to ensure compliance with industry regulations, enhancing their overall security posture.
- **Managed Security Services**: Outsourced certain security functions to a managed security service provider (MSSP) to reduce in-house costs.

- **Scalable Security Solutions:** Invested in scalable cloud-based security solutions to accommodate future growth.

Outcome:

- Achieved compliance with industry standards, enhancing customer trust and opening new business opportunities.
- Reduced the total cost of ownership by outsourcing specialised security tasks.
- Established a scalable security infrastructure that supported the company's rapid growth.

Case Study 3: E-Commerce Startup Prioritises Security Following a Data Breach

Background:

After experiencing a data breach, an e-commerce startup realised the need to revamp its approach to cybersecurity, particularly in protecting customer data.

Strategy:

- **Incident Response Investment**: Invested in developing a robust incident response plan and tools.
- **Data Encryption**: Prioritised budget for encrypting sensitive customer data at rest and in transit.
- **Regular Security Audits**: Allocated funds for regular security audits to identify and address vulnerabilities proactively.

Outcome:

- The incident response plan enabled the company to mitigate and respond to future threats quickly.
- Enhanced data protection measures restored customer confidence.
- Ongoing audits helped continuously improve their security measures and adapt to new threats.

Cybersecurity Spending

Due to often limited resources, cybersecurity spending must be strategically prioritised in a startup environment. The proportion of the expenditure will vary based on the specific needs, size, and nature of the business, but generally, it follows a pattern where critical areas are addressed first. Here's an overview of typical cybersecurity spending in a startup and the general proportion in which the expenditure is made:

1) **Risk Assessment and Management (10-15%)**
   - **Activities**: Identifying vulnerabilities, potential threats, and high-risk areas.
   - **Purpose**: To guide all subsequent cybersecurity investments by prioritising areas of highest risk.

2) **Core Cybersecurity Infrastructure (25-35%)**
   - **Components**: Firewalls, antivirus software, intrusion detection systems.
   - **Purpose**: Establishing a baseline defence to protect against common threats.

3) **Network Security (15-20%)**
   - **Activities**: Implement secure VPNs, wireless networks, and network monitoring tools.
   - **Purpose**: To safeguard data transmission within and outside the organisation.

4) **Identity and Access Management (IAM) (10-15%)**
   - **Tools**: Multi-factor authentication, identity management solutions, access controls.
   - **Purpose**: Ensuring that only authorised individuals can access sensitive systems and data.

5) **Data Encryption (5-10%)**

- **Implementation**: Encrypting data at rest and in transit.
- **Purpose**: Protecting sensitive data from unauthorised access.

6) **Employee Training and Awareness Programs (10-15%)**

- **Activities**: Regular training on cybersecurity best practices and phishing simulations.
- **Purpose**: Minimising risks posed by human error and insider threats.

7) **Incident Response and Recovery (5-10%)**

- **Planning**: Developing and testing incident response plans.
- **Purpose**: Ensuring readiness for and swift response to any cybersecurity incidents.

8) **Compliance and Legal (5-10%)**

- **Activities**: Adhering to relevant industry regulations and data protection laws.
- **Purpose**: Avoid legal penalties and build trust with customers and partners

9) **Continuous Monitoring and Auditing (5-10%)**

- **Tools**: Security Information and Event Management (SIEM) systems, regular security audits.
- **Purpose**: Ongoing oversight and detection of potential security issues.

10) **Miscellaneous and Emerging Technologies (5-10%)**

- **Investments**: Exploring new security technologies and tools, contingency funds.
- **Purpose**: Staying ahead of emerging threats and preparing for unexpected security needs.

The Story of Sam's Cybersecurity Budgeting Strategy for a Fintech Firm

Chapter 1: The Genesis of a Plan

Among innovative startups in the bustling heart of Silicon Valley was a fintech firm known for its cutting-edge financial solutions. However, a critical oversight- cybersecurity- lurked within the surface of its success. This is where Sam, a sharp-witted and visionary IT manager, entered the scene.

Sam had observed how cybersecurity was often sidelined in budget discussions, treated more as an afterthought than a priority. He was determined to change this narrative. He knew that in the fintech world, where vast amounts of sensitive financial data are processed daily, robust cybersecurity was not just an option but a necessity.

Chapter 2: Crafting the Blueprint

Sam started by immersing himself in the company's data flow, identifying where the financial data was most vulnerable. He meticulously charted the journey of sensitive data - from user input to backend processing. His findings were eye-opening; there were gaps in encryption, potential API vulnerabilities, and inadequate intrusion detection systems.

Equipped with this knowledge, Sam began to craft a budget plan. His strategy was not to ask for a blank check but to present a phased investment plan. He broke down the cybersecurity needs into tiers, starting with the most critical areas like encryption and network security, followed by advanced needs like real-time threat detection and AI-based monitoring.

Chapter 3: Winning Over the Board

The real challenge was convincing the board. Sam knew that numbers would speak louder than words. He presented case studies of fintech firms that had suffered devastating losses due to cyberattacks. He highlighted the financial implications, reputational damage, and loss of customer trust.

Sam then showcased his tiered investment plan, outlining how each phase would bolster the firm's security posture and the projected ROI. He emphasised cost-effective solutions, like open-source tools for specific needs, and stressed the importance of employee cybersecurity training, a high-impact yet low-cost measure.

Chapter 4: The Plan in Action

The board was impressed. They approved Sam's plan, commending his foresight and strategic approach. As the plan rolled out, the firm saw significant improvements in its cybersecurity posture. The tiered system allowed flexibility and scalability, adapting to the firm's evolving needs.

Sam's strategy also included regular reviews and audits, ensuring the investments yielded results and adjusting tactics as needed. His focus on employee training paid off, too, as the number of security incidents due to human error dropped dramatically.

Chapter 5: A Model for Others

Sam's success story spread across the fintech industry. His approach to cybersecurity budgeting and investment became a model for other firms, balancing financial prudence with adequate security measures.

In Sam's story, we see the importance of cybersecurity investment and the power of strategic planning, risk assessment, and the ability to articulate the value of security in terms that resonate with decision-makers. His journey transformed the fintech firm's approach to cybersecurity, turning it from a vulnerable startup into a secure, trusted player in the financial sector.

Conclusion

The exact proportions can vary significantly based on the startup's size, industry, regulatory environment, and specific risks. However, the key is ensuring that spending is aligned with the most significant risk and potential impact areas. Startups should also regularly review and adjust their cybersecurity spending as their business and the threat landscape evolve.

Chapter - 5

Talent AcquisitiOn Strategies: Assembling a RObust cybersecurity teamfOrstartups.

Understanding the Cybersecurity Talent Landscape: The Current State of the Job Market in India and the US.

The Global Demand for Cybersecurity Talent

The cybersecurity job market has witnessed exponential growth globally, driven by an increasing number of cyber threats and the adoption of digital technologies across industries. This surge in demand has led to a significant talent gap, as organisations struggle to find skilled professionals to safeguard their digital assets. In the United States, this demand is particularly pronounced. The country, being a hub for technological innovation and home to numerous tech giants, faces a critical shortage of cybersecurity experts. This shortage is not just in technical roles but extends to managerial and strategic cybersecurity positions as well.

Objectives

After studying this chapter, you will understand:

- You will understand the skills requirements in cybersecurity
- How to hire cyber cybersecurity team in startups?

Cybersecurity Talent in India - A Growing Hub

India's cybersecurity job market is growing quickly due to the country's expanding digital economy and its role as a global IT services centre. The Indian government's push for digital projects and the growing awareness of cyber risks among Indian businesses have created a high demand for cybersecurity professionals. Unlike in the US, where the demand is more evenly spread across various roles, India sees a higher demand for entry-level and mid-level cybersecurity professionals. This is partly due to the large number of IT graduates entering the job market each year and the growing number of startups and small businesses requiring cybersecurity services. Additionally, India is becoming a favoured destination for cybersecurity outsourcing, adding another dimension to its job market.

Challenges and Opportunities in Both Markets

Both the US and Indian markets face unique challenges in their quest for cybersecurity talent. In the US, the challenge is more about bridging the skills gap and ensuring a continuous pipeline of trained professionals. In contrast, India's challenge lies in upskilling its vast IT workforce to meet global cybersecurity standards and requirements. However, these challenges also present opportunities: in the US, there is a growing focus on cybersecurity education and training programs, while in India, there is an opportunity to establish itself as a global leader in cybersecurity services. For professionals in both countries, the scenario presents a promising career path, with ample opportunities for growth and learning.

As of 2023, the United States had approximately 1.1 million cybersecurity workers. This figure represents the scale of the cybersecurity workforce in one of the world's largest and most dynamic tech markets. The Bureau of Labour Statistics in the US also reported an expected increase in demand for cybersecurity roles by nearly 35 per cent by 2031, indicating a significant future expansion in this sector.

In India, the cybersecurity job market is rapidly growing, driven by the country's expanding digital economy and a strong IT services sector. As of May 2023, the industry had about 40,000 open opportunities, reflecting the growing demand for skilled cybersecurity professionals in India. However, this also highlights a significant demand-supply gap, with a reported 30 per cent skill challenge in the industry.

This disparity in the number of cybersecurity professionals in both countries underscores the global nature of cybersecurity challenges and the universal need for skilled practitioners in this field.

Identifying Key Security Roles and Skills: Outlining essential roles and skills needed in a cybersecurity team.

Essential Roles in a Cybersecurity Team: In the rapidly evolving field of cybersecurity, the composition of the team is critical. Key roles include–

Chief Information Security Officer (CISO), responsible for overseeing the overall cybersecurity strategy and policies of the organisation.

Security Analysts play a pivotal role in monitoring and analysing the organisation's security posture on a day-to-day basis. They are the front-line defenders, identifying and mitigating threats.

For more technical aspects, Network Security Engineers and Cybersecurity Architects are crucial. They design and maintain secure networks, ensuring the integrity and resilience of network infrastructure.

Incident Response Specialists are trained to handle security breaches and mitigate damage quickly.

Additionally, Ethical Hackers or Penetration Testers are employed to proactively attack systems (with permission) to find vulnerabilities before malicious hackers can exploit them.

As cybersecurity threats have become more sophisticated, roles like AI Security Specialist and Cloud Security Expert have also become essential, focusing on protecting automated and cloud-based environments, respectively.

Key Skills for Cybersecurity Professionals: The skillset required in cybersecurity is diverse and ever-changing. Technical skills such as knowledge of various operating systems, proficiency in programming languages (like Python, Java, or C++), and an understanding of network architecture are fundamental. Equally important is expertise in specific areas like encryption, intrusion detection systems, and firewall management. Soft skills, however, are equally critical. Strong problem-solving abilities enable professionals to tackle complex security challenges effectively. Analytical thinking helps in understanding and mitigating risks, while attention to detail is crucial in identifying subtle signs of security breaches. Communication skills are also key, as cybersecurity professionals often need to explain complex concepts to non-technical stakeholders and lead cross-functional response efforts during incidents.

Additionally, continuous learning is a must in this field, as cybersecurity professionals need to stay abreast of the latest threats, technologies, and compliance regulations.

The Evolving Nature of Cybersecurity Roles: The cybersecurity landscape is dynamic, with emerging technologies continually reshaping the requisite skillsets and roles. For instance, the rise of cloud computing has led to an increased demand for cloud security experts who can navigate the unique challenges of securing cloud environments. Similarly, the growing importance of data privacy and regulatory compliance has given rise to roles specialising in legal and compliance aspects of cybersecurity. As cyber threats become more sophisticated, there is a growing need for professionals skilled in areas like machine learning and artificial intelligence to develop advanced defence mechanisms. This evolving nature of threats and technologies ensures that the field of cybersecurity is not static, requiring professionals to adapt, evolve, and acquire new skills continually.

Expanding further on the skills necessary for cybersecurity professionals:

Technical Skills:

1. **Network Security:** Proficiency in securing network infrastructure, including an understanding of protocols like TCP/IP, DNS, HTTP/HTTPS, and experience with network monitoring tools.
2. **Systems Security**: Knowledge of securing various operating systems such as Windows, Linux, and macOS, including hardening techniques and understanding system vulnerabilities.
3. **Application Security:** Understanding of secure coding practices, application vulnerabilities, and experience with tools for dynamic and static code analysis.
4. **Cloud Security**: Skills in securing cloud environments, including platforms like AWS, Azure, and Google Cloud. Familiarity with cloud-native security tools and best practices for cloud security.

5. **Penetration Testing and Ethical Hacking:** Ability to conduct authorised simulated attacks to identify vulnerabilities in systems, networks, and applications.

6. **Cryptography**: Understanding cryptographic principles, protocols, and the implementation of encryption technologies for data protection.

7. **Security Information and Event Management (SIEM)**: Skills in using SIEM tools for real-time analysis of security alerts generated by applications and network hardware.

8. **Data Privacy and Compliance**: Knowledge of data protection laws and regulations (such as GDPR, HIPAA), and skills in ensuring compliance.

Soft Skills:

1) **Analytical Thinking**

1. Ability to analyse complex security data and logs to discern patterns and identify anomalies that might indicate a security breach.

2. **Problem-Solving:** Skills in developing effective solutions to secure the organisation's digital assets and respond to security incidents.

3. **Communication**: Ability to communicate complex security concepts to non-technical stakeholders and to effectively collaborate with different teams within the organisation.

4. **Attention to Detail:** Vigilance in monitoring security systems and promptly identifying and addressing vulnerabilities and threats.

5. **Adaptability**: Being flexible and able to quickly learn new technologies and adapt to the rapidly evolving cybersecurity landscape.

6. **Leadership and Teamwork:** For higher-level positions, leadership skills are crucial, as well as the ability to work effectively in a team environment.

Emerging Skills:

1. **Machine Learning/AI in Security**: Understanding of how AI and machine learning can be applied for predictive threat modelling and anomaly detection.
2. **IoT Security**: As the number of connected devices grows, skills in securing IoT ecosystems are increasingly important.
3. **Incident Response and Forensics:** Skills in investigating and responding to cybersecurity incidents, including digital forensics.

In the field of cybersecurity, where threats evolve constantly, the willingness and ability to continuously learn and stay updated with the latest trends, tools, and techniques are perhaps the most crucial skills of all. Cybersecurity professionals must balance deep technical knowledge with strong soft skills to effectively protect their organisations against the ever-changing threat landscape.

Effective Recruitment Strategies for Attracting Top Cybersecurity Talent

Creating an Attractive Job Proposition: To attract top cybersecurity talent, companies need to develop compelling job propositions that go beyond competitive salaries. Cybersecurity professionals often seek roles that offer opportunities for growth, challenge, and impact. Emphasise the significance of the role in protecting the company's digital assets and the impact their work will have on the organisation and its clients. Offering professional development opportunities, such as access to advanced training courses or certifications, can also be a major draw. Flexibility is another key factor; considering the current work environment trends, options like remote work or flexible hours can make a position more appealing. Additionally, fostering a company culture that values security, encourages innovation, and supports work-life balance can make the organisation stand out to potential candidates.

Utilizing Multiple Channels for Recruitment

When it comes to recruitment, diversifying the channels used to find candidates can significantly increase the chances of attracting top talent. Traditional job postings on popular job boards are a start, but tapping into industry-specific forums, cybersecurity conferences, and seminars can yield better results. Social media platforms, particularly LinkedIn, can be effective for reaching professionals who may not be actively seeking new opportunities but could be enticed by the right offer. Engaging with local universities and cybersecurity bootcamps can help tap into emerging talent. Additionally, employee referral programs can be particularly effective in this field, as current employees are likely to have connections with skilled professionals in the industry. Offering incentives for successful referrals can motivate employees to recommend qualified candidates.

Building a Strong Employer Brand

A strong employer brand is crucial in attracting top cybersecurity talent. Prospective candidates often research a company's reputation as an employer before applying for or accepting a position. Ensuring that the company is viewed positively in terms of culture, innovation, and employee satisfaction can make a significant difference. Sharing success stories, testimonials from current employees, and insights into the company culture through various media platforms can enhance the employer brand. Participation in industry events, cybersecurity competitions, and webinars can also raise the organisation's profile within the cybersecurity community. Showcasing the company's commitment to cybersecurity, not just as a function but as a core value, can attract professionals who are looking for organisations that take security seriously.

Tailoring the Recruitment Approach to the Startup Ecosystem

For startups in India, developing a targeted recruitment strategy is key to attracting cybersecurity talent. Given the dynamic and often resource-constrained nature of startups, it's important to emphasise the unique opportunities they offer, such as a faster-paced work environment, more diverse responsibilities, and the chance to have a tangible impact on the company's growth and security posture. Startups should highlight their innovative approach, the technologies they work with, and the potential for personal and professional growth. Due to budget constraints, it's also crucial to focus on finding candidates who are not only skilled but also adaptable and willing to grow with the company.

Leveraging Cost-Effective Recruitment Channels

Utilising cost-effective recruitment channels can be particularly beneficial for startups. Engaging with local universities and technical institutes, especially those known for strong IT and cybersecurity programs, can help tap into emerging talent. Participating in hackathons, cybersecurity meetups, and industry conferences can increase visibility among professionals. Social media platforms, particularly LinkedIn and Twitter, can be used to reach a wider audience. Startups should also consider building relationships with incubators and accelerators that often house promising talent. Additionally, employee referrals can be a powerful tool, as existing employees are likely to have networks that include qualified professionals.

Offering Competitive and Creative Compensation Packages

While startups might not always compete with larger corporations in terms of salary, they can offer competitive and creative compensation packages. This could include equity or stock options, which can be a significant draw for employees who want to feel invested in the company's success. Flexible working conditions, opportunities for remote work, and a strong work-life balance can also be attractive. Startups should also focus on creating a strong learning environment offering training programs, certifications, and opportunities to work on cutting-edge projects. Showcasing a culture that values innovation, encourages experimentation, and provides opportunities for employees to take on leadership roles can make a startup more appealing to cybersecurity talent.

Assessing Candidates for Security Roles in Startups-

Evaluating Technical Skills and Experience

When assessing candidates for security roles, the primary focus is on their technical expertise and experience. This involves a thorough review of their knowledge in areas like network security, encryption, threat analysis, and incident response. For specialised roles, proficiency in specific technologies or systems used by your organisation is crucial. Assessing their experience should go beyond just the duration; delve into the complexity and relevance of their previous roles and projects. This can be achieved through technical interviews, practical assessments, or scenario-based questions that challenge candidates to demonstrate their problem-solving abilities and technical acumen. For senior roles, consider their experience in strategising and implementing, and organization - wide security policies.

Soft Skills and Problem-Solving Abilities

Soft skills are equally important in cybersecurity roles. The ability to communicate complex security concepts to non-technical staff, work collaboratively with various teams, and stay calm under pressure are essential traits. Problem-solving skills are critical, as cybersecurity professionals often need to make quick decisions in high-stress situations. During the interview process, ask candidates about past experiences where they had to employ creative problem-solving, handle a crisis, or communicate a technical issue to a non-technical audience. Behavioural interview techniques can be particularly effective in evaluating these skills.

Understanding of Current Cybersecurity Trends and Practices

Given the rapidly evolving nature of cybersecurity threats, a candidate's understanding of current trends and best practices is vital. Assess their knowledge of recent high-profile cyber-attacks, emerging threat vectors, and their views on future security challenges. This can provide insights into their commitment to continuous learning and staying abreast of the industry. Inquire about their participation in professional cybersecurity communities, conferences, and any additional certifications or training they have pursued. This not only shows their dedication to the field but also their ability to bring fresh perspectives and updated knowledge to your team.

Cultural Fit and Adaptability

Finally, assessing how well a candidate fits within your organisation's culture is essential. Cybersecurity teams often work under significant pressure and tight deadlines, making it important for team members to gel well and support each other. Look for candidates who demonstrate adaptability, a willingness to collaborate, and alignment with your company's values and work style. In addition, given the sensitive nature of the work, integrity and trustworthiness are non-negotiable traits. Scenarios or role-play exercises can be useful in assessing these aspects, as well as discussions about ethical dilemmas related to cybersecurity.

Building a Diverse and Inclusive Security

In the field of cybersecurity, diversity is not just a buzzword; it's a strategic advantage. A diverse team, with members from different backgrounds, cultures, genders, and experiences, brings a variety of perspectives that are crucial for out-of-the-box thinking and innovative problem-solving. This diversity is particularly valuable in cybersecurity, where teams face complex and evolving threats that demand creative and varied approaches. To build such a team, organisations need to broaden their recruitment strategies. This includes reaching out to communities and educational institutions with diverse populations, offering internships and training programs to underrepresented groups, and creating inclusive job advertisements that encourage applicants from diverse backgrounds. Partnering with organisations that focus on diversity in STEM can also be a fruitful approach.

Fostering an Inclusive Environment: Attracting diverse talent is only the first step; maintaining an inclusive environment where all team members feel valued and empowered is equally important. This involves creating a workplace culture that respects and celebrates differences, and where every team member has the opportunity to voice their opinions and contribute meaningfully. Regular training sessions on topics like unconscious bias and cultural sensitivity can help in building awareness and fostering inclusivity. Encouraging mentorship programs where seasoned professionals support and guide newcomers from diverse backgrounds can also be highly effective. Moreover, leadership should actively demonstrate their commitment to diversity and inclusivity, setting the tone for the entire organisation.

Measuring Success and Continual Improvement

To ensure the effectiveness of diversity initiatives, it's crucial to measure success and strive for continual improvement. This can involve tracking diversity metrics, such as the representation of different groups at various levels within the security team and soliciting regular feedback from team members on inclusivity issues. It’s also important to recognise and address any barriers to inclusion that may exist within the organisation. Celebrating cultural events, recognising the achievements of team members from diverse backgrounds, and facilitating open and inclusive discussions can contribute to a more positive and productive work environment. By continually striving to enhance diversity and inclusivity, cybersecurity teams can not only enrich their problem - solving capabilities but also mirror the diverse nature of the society they aim to protect.

Training and Development for Security Teams

In the rapidly evolving field of cybersecurity, continuous learning and skill development are crucial for staying ahead of emerging threats. Creating a culture that values and prioritises ongoing education is essential. This can be achieved by implementing regular training sessions, workshops, and webinars that cover the latest cybersecurity trends, technologies, and best practices. Encouraging team members to pursue professional certifications such as CISSP, CISM, or specialised training in areas like ethical hacking, cloud security, or data privacy can greatly enhance their skill sets. Moreover, providing access to online learning platforms like Coursera, Udemy, or industry-specific resources can offer flexible learning opportunities tailored to individual needs.

Personal Development Plans and Skill Assessments

Developing personalised training and development plans for each team member can be highly effective. This involves conducting regular skill assessments to identify areas where each team member can improve or expand their expertise. Based on these assessments, personalised development plans can be created, which may include mentorship programs, cross-training within the team, or specialised external courses. Recognising and rewarding progress and achievements in training can also motivate team members to engage actively in their professional development. Regularly updating these plans ensures they remain relevant and aligned with both the individual's career goals and the organisation's evolving security needs.

Leveraging External Resources and Partnerships

No cybersecurity team can operate in isolation, nor can it possess expertise in every aspect of this diverse field. Leveraging external resources and partnerships can significantly enhance a team's capabilities. This can involve engaging with cybersecurity consultants for specialised knowledge, contracting external security firms for specific tasks like penetration testing, or using managed security services for continuous monitoring and threat detection. Participating in cybersecurity forums, industry groups, and professional networks can provide access to a wealth of knowledge and resources, including threat intelligence, best practices, and the latest research in the field.

Collaborative Partnerships and Information Sharing

Forming collaborative partnerships with other organisations, including competitors, can be beneficial. Participating in information-sharing consortia or industry-specific security alliances allows teams to share threat intelligence, experiences, and strategies, enhancing collective defence capabilities. Collaborating with academic institutions or research organisations can provide insights into cutting-edge security research and emerging technologies. Additionally, public-private partnerships can offer opportunities to collaborate on broader security initiatives and contribute to developing industry standards and regulations.

Late Night Discovery: Balancing Cybersecurity in a Thriving Fintech Startup

Late Night Discovery

Ramesh, a highly skilled cybersecurity professional and the CTO of a flourishing fintech company in Bangalore, was working late one night when he noticed unusual activity on the company's network. The systems, typically efficient and uninterrupted, were behaving erratically. With his keen eye for detail and deep understanding of cyber threats, Ramesh quickly realised they were potentially under attack. Diving into the logs and analysing the network traffic, his suspicions were confirmed: malware had infiltrated the system.

The Lone Warrior's Nightlong Battle

Ramesh, though alarmed, maintained his composure, understanding the responsibility resting on his shoulders. He embarked on a nightlong mission, meticulously working to eradicate the malware and reinforce the company's cybersecurity defences. Collaborating remotely with the IT team, he updated the firewall, blocked suspicious activities, and closely monitored the systems. By dawn, Ramesh's efforts had paid off; the threat was neutralised, and the systems were restored to normal. Though physically exhausted, the sense of achievement and pride he felt was unparalleled – he had single-handedly averted a potential disaster.

Building a Hybrid Cybersecurity Strategy

Despite this victory, Ramesh knew that a more sustainable solution was needed for the long-term security of his company. Faced with the decision of whether to build an internal cybersecurity team or outsource the function, Ramesh chose a hybrid approach. He planned to form a robust in-house team while also leveraging the expertise of an external security consultant. This strategy would combine the control and dedicated focus of an internal team with the broader perspective and experience of an external advisor.

Assembling a Team of Experts

The recruitment process was rigorous. Ramesh sought individuals who were not only cybersecurity experts but also adept at staying ahead of rapidly evolving cyber threats. Eventually, he assembled a team of exceptional talents, each bringing unique skills and insights to the table. Together with the external consultant, they developed a comprehensive cybersecurity plan encompassing employee training, regular vulnerability assessments, and advanced security software implementation.

Securing the Future

The new cybersecurity strategy proved to be highly effective. The company strengthened its defences, safeguarding its data and systems against emerging cyber threats. Ramesh's decision to combine internal expertise with external guidance had paid off, providing a multifaceted approach to cybersecurity. The story of Ramesh and his fintech company became a testament to the importance of proactive cybersecurity measures and the power of a well-rounded, adaptive approach in the digital age.

Summary and Recruitment Guide for a Startup's Cybersecurity Team

Ramesh's experience with his fintech startup underscores the indispensable role of cybersecurity in today's digital business world. His story illuminates the need for relentless vigilance, illustrates the effectiveness of a combined internal and external cybersecurity strategy, and emphasises the importance of assembling a team that is both skilled and adaptable to the fast-paced changes in the cyber threat landscape.

Step-by-Step Hiring Process for Cybersecurity Professionals

1) Identifying Hiring Needs:

Begin by pinpointing the specific cybersecurity roles and skills that your startup needs. Assess the areas where your company is most vulnerable and what expertise is required to fortify these aspects.

2) Posting Job Listings:

Utilise professional platforms like LinkedIn or Indeed to post job listings. These sites allow you to reach a broad audience of qualified candidates. Ensure that your job descriptions are clear, detailed, and highlight the unique opportunities and challenges of working in a startup environment.

3) Application Review and Shortlisting:

Carefully review applications to identify candidates whose qualifications align with your needs. Look for a blend of technical skills, experience, and potential cultural fit with your startup's ethos.

4) Conducting Interviews:

During interviews, focus on understanding the candidate's experience, technical acumen, and problem-solving skills.

Observe their body language and demeanour to gauge their communication skills and how they might fit into the team.

Pose questions that challenge their problem-solving abilities and assess their capacity for teamwork and collaboration.

5) Making a Job Offer:

Once you have identified your preferred candidate, extend a job offer. This should include a comprehensive offer letter detailing the role, responsibilities, salary, and benefits.

Clearly communicate the growth opportunities and unique advantages of joining a startup.

6) Building a Hybrid Cybersecurity Team:

Remember Ramesh's approach: complement your internal team with external expertise. Consider hiring a security consultant for broader strategic input and access to specialised knowledge.

By following these steps, startups can effectively build a cybersecurity team that not only protects the company from digital threats but also contributes to its overall innovation and growth. Ramesh's successful approach serves as a model for startups navigating the complex and crucial domain of cybersecurity.

Deciding Between Hiring Employees and Engaging Consultants for a Startup

In the dynamic environment of a startup, especially when developing a cybersecurity strategy, adopting a hybrid approach that combines hiring key personnel with engaging consultants can be highly effective. Initially, hiring a Virtual Chief Information Security Officer (vCISO) is a strategic move. A vCISO brings in expert knowledge and leadership in cybersecurity without the financial burden of a full-time executive hire. This role is pivotal in crafting a tailored cybersecurity strategy, identifying critical areas of risk, and setting the foundation for the company's security posture. The vCISO can work closely with the CTO and other executives to ensure that cybersecurity is integrated into the overall business strategy. They play a shepherd-like role, guiding the company through the initial stages of building its cybersecurity framework.

Balancing the Team with Security Engineers and Consultants

Alongside a vCISO, hiring one or two security engineers can form the core of the cybersecurity team. These engineers would be responsible for the day-to-day implementation of the cybersecurity plan under the guidance of the vCISO. Their roles would involve active monitoring of security systems, managing incident responses, and maintaining the security infrastructure. However, due to the diverse and ever-evolving nature of cybersecurity threats, relying solely on in-house expertise might limit the startup's capabilities. This is where engaging with external cybersecurity consultants becomes advantageous. Consultants can bring a diverse skill set and specialised expertise that might not be available in-house. They can provide insights into industry best practices, offer training to the internal team, and help in tackling specific cybersecurity challenges. Engaging consultants is also cost-effective, allowing the startup to access high-level expertise on an as-needed basis without committing to the overhead costs of a full-time specialist.

Pros of Engaging Cybersecurity Consultants

1. **Expertise on Demand**: Consultants provide access to a wide range of specialised skills and knowledge that can be tapped into as required.
2. **Cost-Effectiveness:** Hiring consultants can be more economical, especially for short-term projects or specific tasks, reducing the need for full-time specialised staff.
3. **Objective Insights:** External consultants can offer unbiased perspectives on the company's cybersecurity posture, free from internal politics or biases.
4. **Scalability and Flexibility:** As the startup grows and its needs evolve, consultants can be engaged to address specific areas without the long-term commitment of hiring additional staff.
5. **Keeping Pace with Industry Trends:** Consultants, being active in various environments and industries, can bring in fresh insights and knowledge of the latest cybersecurity trends and threats.

For startups looking to fortify their cybersecurity posture, a balanced and strategic approach is key. Integrating a Virtual CISO, a dedicated team of security engineers, and selectively engaging external cybersecurity consultants can establish a comprehensive and adaptable cybersecurity strategy. This model not only lays the groundwork for a robust security infrastructure but also ensures the flexibility to navigate and respond to the evolving challenges and innovations in the cybersecurity arena.

Selecting the Ideal Security Lead

1) Identifying the Right Blend of Skills:

When making your initial security hire, it's crucial to find someone who possesses both technical acumen and strong interpersonal skills. The ideal candidate should be adept at the technical aspects of information security while also being comfortable in communicating with various stakeholders, both within and outside the organisation.

2) Role of the Security Lead in Stakeholder Engagement:

For instance, if a customer has concerns about product security, the security lead should be capable of working collaboratively with the sales team. They must effectively translate customer feedback into practical insights for product development, ensuring that security considerations are seamlessly integrated into the product lifecycle.

3) Essential Qualities and Expertise:

The security lead should exhibit a comprehensive set of qualities and skills, including:

Technical expertise in information security.

Strong problem-solving skills and a proactive approach to security challenges.

Strategic thinking and an understanding of the broader business landscape.

Familiarity with industry best practices in cybersecurity. Proficiency in security operations and incident response.

Attention to detail and the ability to remain composed under pressure.

4) The Search for the Right Candidate:

Finding such a multifaceted individual is undoubtedly challenging but critical for the role. If you're uncertain about where to begin, consider tapping into your professional network or seeking assistance from IT staffing agencies specialising in cybersecurity roles.

In essence, the success of a startup's cybersecurity efforts hinges on the ability to assemble a well-rounded team led by a competent and versatile security lead. This individual not only needs to have the technical know - how but also the soft skills necessary for effective communication and collaboration across different levels of the organisation. With the right team in place, startups can navigate the complexities of the cybersecurity landscape with confidence and resilience.

Building and Structuring a Cybersecurity Team in Your Organisation

Building a cybersecurity team that effectively safeguards your organisation requires a strategic approach to team composition. The structure and focus of your cybersecurity team should align with your organisation's specific needs, industry demands, and the type of digital assets you need to protect. Here are key components of a well-rounded cybersecurity team:

1) Cloud Security Team:

Role: This team specialises in securing your organisation's cloud-based infrastructure and services. They are experts in implementing and managing network security tools, firewalls, and intrusion detection/prevention systems, specifically in cloud environments.

Recruitment Focus: Look for professionals with 2-3 years of experience in cloud security, particularly those with expertise in platforms like AWS, Azure, or GCP. Candidates should possess a strong grasp of cloud security principles and technologies.

2) Incident Response Team:

Role: Tasked with managing and responding to cybersecurity incidents, this team plays a critical role in identifying, investigating, containing, and remediating security breaches.

Team Skills: Assemble a group skilled in forensic analysis, crisis management, and effective communication. This team should be adept at quickly diagnosing problems and implementing solutions to minimise damage and restore systems.

3) Application Security Team:

Role: Focused on securing all software applications, this team works to identify and remediate vulnerabilities throughout the software development lifecycle.

Expertise Required: Recruit individuals with experience in secure coding practices, code review, and vulnerability testing. Their goal is to proactively address security flaws to prevent potential exploits and data breaches.

4) Threat Intelligence Team:

Role: This team is responsible for staying ahead of emerging threats by gathering and analysing intelligence about potential risks to the organisation's security posture.

Skills Needed: Team members should be proficient in data analysis, threat modeling and have a deep understanding of the current cyber threat landscape. They provide critical insights to inform security strategies and defensive measures.

5) Governance, Risk Management, and Compliance (GRC) Team:

Role: This team ensures the organisation adheres to regulatory and industry compliance standards. They develop and enforce policies and procedures to maintain compliance and manage risk.

Qualifications: Look for individuals with expertise in legal, regulatory standards, internal audits, and risk assessment. They should be knowledgeable about the specific compliance requirements pertinent to your industry.

Designing Your Cybersecurity Team:

Assess Your Needs: Start by assessing your organisation's specific security needs. Consider factors like the size of your organisation, the nature of your data, and your digital infrastructure.

Balanced Team Structure: Aim for a balanced team structure with a mix of skills and experiences. Include both technical and managerial roles to ensure comprehensive coverage of all cybersecurity aspects.

Continuous Training: Invest in continuous training and development for your team to keep them updated with the latest security trends and technologies.

Collaborative Environment: Foster a collaborative environment where different teams work together to ensure a holistic security approach.

Incorporating these diverse teams into your cybersecurity strategy will provide a comprehensive defence mechanism against a wide range of cyber threats. Each team plays a unique and critical role in protecting the organisation, and its coordinated efforts will strengthen your overall security posture.

Chapter - 6
Cultivating A Security-Aware Culture

Cultivating a Security-Aware Culture

"There are two types of companies: those that have been hacked, and those who don't yet know they have been hacked."

-John Chambers (former CEO of Cisco)

In the contemporary digital landscape, where cyber threats loom large, the importance of security awareness extends far beyond the confines of the IT department. In this chapter, we'll look at the importance of security awareness and how to foster a security-aware culture in companies. This chapter will serve as a complete guide for technology professionals, security experts and executives to instil a cybersecurity culture within an organisation. By fostering a security-conscious culture, businesses can significantly mitigate risks, fortify defences, and empower their workforce to proactively combat cyber threats.

Objectives

After studying this chapter, you will understand:

- Importance of security awareness
- Why is security awareness the most important defence?
- How does security awareness play a crucial role in mitigating insider threats?

Importance of Security Awareness

The Universal Relevance of Security Awareness

In the contemporary digital landscape, where cyber threats loom large, the importance of security awareness extends far beyond the confines of the IT department. Every employee, irrespective of their role, is a potential entry point for cyber threats, making it critical for everyone in the organisation to be vigilant and informed. Security awareness is not just about understanding the technicalities of cyber-attacks but also recognising the role each individual plays in the organisation's defensive matrix. This section of the book emphasises how fostering a culture of security awareness among all employees is not a luxury but a necessity.

It is about transforming every staff member from a potential security risk into an informed, proactive defender of the organisation's digital assets.

Reducing Vulnerabilities Through Education

One of the most effective weapons against cyber threats is knowledge. Educating employees about common cyber threats like phishing, social engineering, malware, and ransomware empowers them to recognise and avoid these dangers. Regular training sessions, security briefings, and simulations of potential security scenarios play a pivotal role in this educational process. This book will delve into how a well-informed workforce can act as a formidable first line of defence, significantly reducing the organisation's vulnerability to attacks. By embedding security awareness into the organisational culture, companies can transform their employees from the weakest link in the security chain into a robust and first line of defence.

Safeguarding Digital Assets Through Collective Vigilance

The final aim of fostering security awareness is to protect the organisation's invaluable digital assets. In a world where data breaches can result in substantial financial losses and irreparable reputational damage, the stakes are incredibly high. This book underscores the point that while advanced cybersecurity tools and protocols are essential, the human element cannot be overlooked. It will explore how a security-conscious workforce, equipped with the knowledge and tools to identify and respond to threats, can fortify the organisation's defences. Through collective vigilance and a shared commitment to security, organisations can not only prevent breaches but also quickly mitigate any damage should an incident occur.

Why Security Awareness is Still the Most Important Defence?

1. **Human Factor as the Primary Vulnerability**: Despite advanced technologies, human error remains a leading cause of security breaches. Educated employees can recognise and avoid potential threats, reducing the risk of successful attacks.

2. **Evolving Nature of Cyber Threats**: Cyber threats are continually evolving. Regular security awareness training helps employees stay updated on the latest tactics used by cybercriminals, such as new phishing schemes or social engineering tactics.

3. **Prevention is Better Than Cure**: It is more cost-effective to prevent security incidents than to deal with their consequences. A well-informed workforce can prevent breaches, saving the organisation from financial loss and reputational damage.

4. **Compliance with Regulations**: Many data protection and privacy regulations, such as GDPR, require employee training as part of compliance. Security awareness ensures that employees understand their role in maintaining compliance.

5. **Empowering Employees**: Security awareness empowers employees to take responsibility for their actions and understand the impact of their behaviour on the organisation's security.

6. **Building a Security Culture**: Continuous security training fosters a culture of security within the organisation. This culture is critical in ensuring that security considerations are part of everyday business processes.

7. **Rapid Response to Incidents**: Employees trained in security awareness can respond more quickly and effectively to potential security incidents, reducing the potential damage.

8. **Widespread Use of Digital Technologies**: As more business processes move online, the potential for cyber threats increases. Security awareness is crucial in ensuring that employees use these technologies safely.

9. **Insider Threat Mitigation**: Security awareness training can help in identifying and mitigating insider threats, whether malicious or

unintentional.

10. **Public Perception and Trust**: Companies known for taking cybersecurity seriously are more likely to be trusted by customers and partners. Security awareness among employees enhances this trust.

11. **Protecting Remote Workforce**: With the rise of remote work, employees are more isolated from the IT department. Security awareness is essential in ensuring they maintain security practices outside the office environment.

Cybersecurity Statistics

Global statistics on insider cyber-attacks highlight the significant and growing challenge they pose:

- **Prevalence of Insider Threats**: Approximately 31% of all data breaches in the last year were caused by insider threats, including insiders, contractors, or employees. The average global cost of an insider threat is a staggering $8.76 million, factoring in tarnished reputations, legal expenses, and lost data costs.
- **Growth Rate**: Insider attacks have grown by over 47% in the past two years, influenced by factors like the rise of cloud computing, mobile device usage, and social media platforms.
- **Negligence as a Key Factor**: Over two-thirds of insider threat incidents result from negligence, highlighting the importance of employee training and awareness in mitigating these risks.
- **Challenges in the Cloud**: Detecting insider attacks is becoming increasingly difficult in cloud environments, with over 53% of survey respondents acknowledging this challenge.
- **Credential Theft**: Around 61% of all attacks involve credential theft, whether through brute force hacking or social engineering.
- **Human Error**: Over 91.5% of cyber-attacks are attributed to human mistakes, underscoring the critical role of human factors in cybersecurity.

How Security Awareness Helps in Mitigating Insider Threats?

Security awareness plays a crucial role in mitigating insider threats, which are security risks originating from within the organisation. These risks can be intentional (such as malicious activities by disgruntled employees) or unintentional (like accidental data breaches due to negligence). Here's how security awareness can help:

1. **Educating Employees About Insider Threat Indicators**: Training sessions can inform employees about the signs of potential insider threats. This includes unusual system access, unauthorised data transfers, and suspicious behaviour by colleagues. Awareness enables employees to recognise and report such activities promptly.

2. **Fostering a Security Culture**: By instilling a strong security culture, employees understand the importance of following best practices and policies. This reduces the likelihood of careless behaviour that could lead to unintentional insider threats.

3. **Minimising Malicious Insider Activities**: Regular awareness training can deter potential malicious insiders. When employees are aware that their colleagues are educated and vigilant, they understand that malicious activities are more likely to be detected and reported.

4. **Enhancing Reporting Mechanisms**: Security awareness training typically includes information on how to report suspicious activities. Employees who are confident about reporting procedures are more likely to come forward with critical information about potential insider threats.

5. **Empowering Employees with Knowledge**: Well-informed employees are less likely to be exploited by malicious insiders. For example, an employee aware of the dangers of social engineering will be less likely to divulge sensitive information to someone manipulating them under pretences.

6. **Regular Reminders and Updates**: Continuous security awareness efforts ensure that the information stays fresh in employees' minds, reminding them to always be vigilant and cautious in their daily activities.

7. **Promoting a Shared Responsibility for Security**: When all employees understand that security is not just the IT department's responsibility but everyone's, it creates an environment where insider threats are less likely to thrive.

Now we can look at what are how organisations can keep their employee trained and aware of cybersecurity

Building Cyber Security Awareness

Regular Awareness Sessions: Emphasise the importance of conducting regular sessions that update employees on the latest cyber threats and best practices.

- **Objectives and Content:** The primary objective of these sessions is to keep the workforce abreast of the ever-changing landscape of cyber threats. The content should include, but not be limited to, updates on recent cyber incidents, trends in phishing tactics, and insights into the mechanisms of ransomware or other malware attacks. It is also vital to cover changes in company policies, compliance requirements, and the introduction of new security tools or protocols.
- **Frequency and Format:** The frequency of these sessions should reflect the pace at which cyber threats evolve; quarterly sessions are a recommended minimum, with monthly updates being ideal for industries facing higher threat levels. The format should be engaging, utilising various multimedia tools such as videos, interactive quizzes, and real-world case studies to illustrate the impact of cyber threats.
- **Customisation for Relevance:** Sessions must be tailored to address the specific roles and responsibilities of different groups within the organisation. For example, the finance department might receive detailed training on the latest methods of fraud, while the IT department might delve deeper into technical defences against system breaches.
- **Expert Speakers and Workshops**: Bringing in external cybersecurity experts for guest lectures can provide fresh perspectives and credibility to the information shared. Workshops that allow employees to practice what they've learned in a controlled environment can be particularly effective for skills retention.

- **Measuring Effectiveness:** The effectiveness of these sessions can be gauged through post-session assessments and the monitoring of cybersecurity incidents within the organisation. Feedback from employees should be solicited to improve future sessions and ensure that they remain relevant and engaging.
- **Continuous Improvement:** The content of awareness sessions should be continually reviewed and updated to reflect the latest threats and security practices. This requires a dedicated effort from the cybersecurity team to stay informed and creative in their approach to education.

Customised Training Content: Tailor training content to different departments, recognising that different roles have varied levels of exposure and different risk profiles.

Leadership Involvement: Leadership involvement is a critical factor in the success of cybersecurity awareness initiatives within any organisation. When leaders champion cybersecurity efforts, it sends a clear message about the importance of secure practices and establishes a tone of vigilance from the top down.

- **Setting the Precedent:** Leaders must set a precedent by adhering to the same security protocols they expect of their employees. Their behaviour should exemplify the organisation's commitment to cybersecurity. This includes using strong passwords, participating in training sessions, and demonstrating a thorough understanding of the organisation's cyber risk profile.
- **Visible Endorsement:** Top management can reinforce the seriousness of cybersecurity initiatives by visibly endorsing them. This can take the form of opening or closing remarks at training sessions, written communications stressing the importance of cybersecurity, and recognition of employees who exemplify best practices.
- **Resource Allocation:** Leadership must ensure that adequate resources are allocated to cybersecurity training and infrastructure. This includes budgeting for regular updates to training materials, investment in security technologies, and hiring of personnel dedicated to cybersecurity roles.

- **Incorporating Cybersecurity in Corporate Values:** Incorporating cybersecurity into the organisation's core values can cement its importance within the company culture. Leadership should advocate for cybersecurity to be seen as a fundamental aspect of corporate responsibility and ethics.
- **Leadership Training**: Top executives should receive specialised training that covers the specific cybersecurity risks associated with their decision-making roles. Understanding the strategic implications of cyber threats enables them to make more informed decisions about policies and initiatives.
- **Communicating with Stakeholders:** Leaders are often the primary communicators with external stakeholders. They should be prepared to discuss the organisation's cybersecurity stance and how it protects customer and partner data. Transparency about cybersecurity efforts can enhance trust and reputation.
- **Crisis Management:** In the event of a cybersecurity incident, leadership must be prepared to manage the situation effectively. This involves not only addressing the immediate technical challenges but also communicating with employees, customers, and the public to maintain confidence in the organisation's ability to handle such events.
- **Continuous Engagement:** Finally, leaders should be continuously engaged with the cybersecurity team, staying updated on the latest threats and the effectiveness of the training program. Their ongoing involvement can drive continuous improvement in cybersecurity practices.

Innovative Training Methods

- **Interactive Phishing Simulations**: Discuss the effectiveness of simulated phishing attacks in training employees to recognise and report potential threats.
- **Gamification**: Elaborate on how gamifying cybersecurity training can increase engagement and retention of information. Examples could include reward systems, leaderboards, and interactive challenges.
- **Information Privacy Week (IP Week)**: Designating a special week for intensive cybersecurity education can have a substantial impact on an organisation's security posture. This focused

approach, often termed 'Cybersecurity Awareness Week' or 'Information Privacy Week', combines structured learning sessions, interactive workshops, and keynote speeches from industry experts to create a dynamic learning environment.

- **Structured Learning Sessions:** The week can begin with structured sessions that provide foundational knowledge on cybersecurity topics. These sessions should be designed to cater to varying levels of expertise within the organisation and might include basics of cybersecurity hygiene, advanced threat modelling, or secure coding practices for developers.
- **Interactive Workshops:** Workshops provide hands-on experience with real-world scenarios. Employees can participate in incident response drills, phishing simulations, or secure password creation exercises. This practical approach helps solidify learning and demonstrates the application of concepts in a controlled, risk-free environment.
- **Guest Speakers and Panels:** Inviting guest speakers, such as cybersecurity experts, law enforcement officials specialising in cybercrimes, or victims of cyber incidents, can offer diverse perspectives. Panel discussions on current cyber threats, trends, and debates can provoke thought and discussion among employees, fostering a deeper understanding of the issues at hand.
- **Focused Themes:** Each day of the week can be dedicated to a specific theme, such as 'Social Engineering', 'Network Security', or 'Mobile Device Protection'. This thematic approach ensures comprehensive coverage of various cybersecurity domains and keeps the content organised and engaging.
- **Employee Engagement and Recognition:** Throughout the week, employees can be encouraged to engage in cybersecurity challenges, quizzes, or competitions with rewards for participation and achievement. Recognising individuals or departments that have made significant contributions to the organisation's cybersecurity reinforces the importance of everyone's involvement.

- **Exhibition and Technology Demos:** A showcase of the latest cybersecurity technologies by vendors can provide insights into the practical tools available to defend against cyber threats. Live demos can illustrate the sophistication of cybersecurity solutions and their role in protecting organisational assets.
- **Feedback and Follow-Up:** Gathering feedback at the end of each session and at the week's conclusion is crucial for assessing the effectiveness of the event. Follow-up materials and resources can be distributed to reinforce key messages and encourage ongoing learning.
- **Use of Virtual and Augmented Reality**: Explore how VR and AR can create immersive learning experiences for complex cybersecurity concepts.

Leveraging New Technologies

- **Artificial Intelligence and Machine Learning**: Discuss how AI and ML can be used in predictive analytics to identify potential phishing attempts or abnormal user behaviour.
- **Mobile Learning Applications**: Suggest the use of mobile apps for flexible, on-the-go training that can reach employees anytime, anywhere.
- **Advanced Reporting Tools**: Mention how data analytics tools can assess the effectiveness of the training programs, helping to identify areas for improvement.
- **Data Security Strategies**: For startups, data security is critical to safeguard customer information, intellectual property, financial records, and other sensitive assets from cyber threats and compliance violations. It includes controls like encryption, access management, DLP (Data Loss Prevention), secure backups, and regular auditing to ensure that only authorised individuals can access or manipulate the data.

Data security solutions from ManageEngine

ManageEngine's data security solutions enable startups to protect sensitive information, meet regulatory compliance requirements, and turn customer trust into a lasting competitive edge.

- **Data leak prevention:** Detect, disrupt, and prevent sensitive data leaks via endpoints, i.e., USBs, emails, print, and more, through real-time security monitoring.
- **Data risk assessment:** Locate sensitive data and analyse its vulnerability with data risk assessment.
- **File server auditing:** Seamlessly monitor, alert, and report on all file accesses and modifications made across Windows file servers, failover clusters, workgroups, and NetApp CIFS servers.
- **Cloud protection:** Track the organisation's web traffic and enforce policies to safeguard employees against inappropriate or malicious web content.
- **Ransomware detection:** Detect and shut down ransomware attacks at inception with an automated threat response mechanism, and get notified with instant, user-defined alerts.

Key products: DataSecurity Plus, Endpoint DLP Plus, Device Control Plus, Ransomware Protection Plus and Malware Protection Plus

Visit: www.manageengine.com/dlp to know more.

Conclusion

DevOps engineers and software developers play a crucial role in maintaining cybersecurity, and there are several effective ways for them to enhance their security awareness. One of the most engaging methods is through participation in 'Capture the Flag' (CTF) competitions. These contests offer practical, hands-on cybersecurity challenges that range from solving puzzles to breaking into systems or defending them. CTFs not only sharpen technical skills but also provide insights into the mindset of attackers.

Leading platforms for such learning include Hack the Box, CTFd, and Over the Wire, which are renowned for their comprehensive and challenging scenarios. Additionally, online learning platforms like Cybrary, Coursera, and Udemy offer specialised courses in cybersecurity, providing theoretical knowledge and practical skills. By utilising these resources, DevOps engineers and software developers can significantly improve their understanding of security threats and best practices, thereby contributing to the overall security posture of their organisations.

Chapter - 7

LOOking tO The Future

Emerging Cybersecurity Trends

"There's no silver bullet with cybersecurity; a layered defense is the only viable option."

- James Scott

As we delve into the heart of the future of cybersecurity, it becomes increasingly clear that this landscape is rapidly evolving, driven by technological advancements and changing threat paradigms. This section will explore the latest trends shaping this dynamic field, focusing on two pivotal developments: quantum computing and IoT (Internet of Things) security. These emerging trends are not mere shifts in technology but represent fundamental changes in how we perceive and defend against cyber threats.

Objectives

After studying this chapter, you will understand:

- The future of cybersecurity
- Emerging risks and challenges
- Impact of changing privacy laws

Key Statistics and Insights

The future of cybersecurity is marked by a range of emerging risks and challenges, as highlighted by several recent reports and studies. Here are some key statistics and insights from these sources:

1) ISACA's 2023 State of Cybersecurity Report:

In this report, it was noted that 48% of organisations reported an increase in cyberattacks compared to the previous year. Although this figure is concerning, it represents the smallest reported increase in cyberattacks over the past six years.

2) Kaspersky's 2023 Cybersecurity Landscape Analysis: Kaspersky's experts have highlighted the profound influence of artificial intelligence (AI) on the cybersecurity landscape in 2023. Their analysis delves into how AI is being used by both defenders and regulators, as well as its potential exploitation by cybercriminals, indicating a multifaceted impact of AI on cybersecurity.

3) Risk Lens' 2023 Cybersecurity Risk Report:

This report provides in-depth insights from Cyber Risk Quantification (CRQ) experts on top cyber risk scenarios, loss exposure by industry, and threat categories. It also includes an analysis of total loss exposure, event probability, and the financial impact of key cyber events from the previous year.

4) World Economic Forum's Global Cybersecurity Outlook 2023: According to this report, 86% of business leaders and 93% of cyber leaders believe that global geopolitical instability is likely to lead to a catastrophic cyber event in the next two years. This highlights the growing concern among leaders about the potential for significant cyber incidents in the near future.

5) Cybersecurity Ventures' 2023 Predictions:

Cybersecurity Ventures predicts that cybercrime is set to inflict damages totalling USD 8 trillion globally in 2023. If measured as a country, cybercrime would rank as the world's third-largest economy after the U.S. and China, underscoring the massive scale and impact of cyber threats.

Now, let's look at some of the future cybersecurity risks and their implications.

Quantum Computing and Cybersecurity

The advent of quantum computing poses a double-edged sword for cybersecurity. On the one hand, quantum computers, with their immense processing power, promise breakthroughs in various fields, including cryptography. Traditional encryption methods, which form the backbone of current cybersecurity practices, may become obsolete in the face of quantum computing's ability to solve complex algorithms at unprecedented speeds. This necessitates a paradigm shift in cryptographic methods, steering towards quantum-resistant algorithms. On the other hand, quantum computing offers new horizons in cybersecurity defence mechanisms. Its ability to quickly analyse massive datasets can revolutionise threat detection and response strategies, leading to more robust and adaptive security systems. The balance between these two aspects of quantum computing will define a significant part of cybersecurity's future.

Risk in Quantum Computing

Breaking Current Cryptographic Standards:

- Quantum computers have the potential to break widely used cryptographic algorithms, such as RSA and ECC, which are based on the difficulty of factoring large numbers or solving discrete logarithm problems.
- This capability could compromise the security of current encryption methods used for protecting sensitive data, including financial transactions, government communications, and personal data.
- Organisations and governments may find their encrypted data exposed unless they transition to quantum-resistant cryptographic methods.

Data Harvesting for Future Decryption:

- Adversaries could collect encrypted data with the intention of decrypting it once quantum computing becomes sufficiently advanced.

- This strategy, known as "harvest now, decrypt later," poses a long-term threat to data currently considered secure.

Impact on Blockchain and Digital Currencies:

- Many blockchain technologies and digital currencies, like Bitcoin, rely on cryptographic algorithms vulnerable to quantum attacks.
- The advent of quantum computing could undermine the integrity and security of blockchain systems, potentially leading to unauthorised transactions and access to wallets.

Increased Complexity in Cybersecurity:

- The introduction of quantum-resistant algorithms will require a complete overhaul of existing security infrastructure.
- Organisations will face challenges in implementing these new algorithms, including compatibility issues, increased computational requirements, and the need for widespread updates to hardware and software.

Quantum Attacks on Secure Communications:

- Quantum computing may enable new forms of cyber-attacks that could intercept or disrupt secure communications, posing a threat to national security and critical infrastructure.
- Governments and intelligence agencies may need to revise their communication methods to counteract these potential quantum-based eavesdropping techniques.
- The impact of quantum computing on blockchain technologies and digital currencies such as Bitcoin is a subject of growing concern in the cryptographic and financial communities.

The primary issue lies in the vulnerability of current cryptographic algorithms to potential quantum attacks. Here's an expanded view of this topic:

Vulnerability of Cryptographic Algorithms:

- Blockchain and digital currencies like Bitcoin rely heavily on cryptographic algorithms such as SHA-256 and ECDSA (Elliptic

Curve Digital Signature Algorithm) for security.

- Quantum computers, with their ability to perform complex calculations at incredible speeds, could theoretically break these algorithms.
- For instance, Shor's algorithm, a quantum algorithm, can factor large numbers and compute discrete logarithms, tasks that are foundational to the security of most cryptographic algorithms used today.

Risk to Bitcoin and Other Cryptocurrencies:

- Bitcoin's security, for instance, is predicated on the difficulty of solving some mathematical issues, which are currently infeasible for classical computers.
- Quantum computers could solve these problems much more rapidly, jeopardising the security of Bitcoin transactions and wallet security.
- This could lead to scenarios where a quantum-enabled attacker could forge transactions or steal Bitcoin by deriving private keys from public keys.

Impact on Blockchain Integrity:

- Blockchain's integrity is based on the security of its blocks, which are cryptographically chained together.
- A quantum computer could potentially alter the contents of a block and recompute the Proof of Work for that block and all subsequent blocks quickly, leading to a potential rewriting of the blockchain.
- This undermines the fundamental principle of immutability in blockchain technology, which is critical for its trust and reliability.

Future of Digital Currency Security:

To counter the looming quantum threats, new quantum-resistant cryptographic algorithms are being developed, specifically designed to withstand the advanced capabilities of quantum computers. As blockchain and digital currency platforms heavily rely on cryptographic security, they will need to adopt these new algorithms to protect their systems from potential quantum attacks. This transition is not simple and will require a coordinated effort across the industry, posing significant technical and logistical challenges. Currently, the scientific consensus is that practical quantum computers capable of breaking today's cryptographic systems are still several years away. However, the threat is severe enough that planning and preparation for quantum-resistant technologies need to start now to stay ahead of potential risks.

Some forward-thinking blockchain projects are already exploring quantum-resistant technologies, employing cryptographic methods believed to be secure against quantum computing attacks. These technologies are still in the development phase, and their successful adoption will be crucial for the long-term viability of blockchain and digital currencies. Governments and international organisations might need to play a significant role in standardizing and regulating this transition, ensuring a uniform approach to security and preventing fragmentation in how different blockchain platforms respond to the quantum threat.

There are concerns that if a few entities monopolise quantum computing technology, it could lead to an imbalance in computational power, granting unfair advantages in fields like military applications, intelligence, and economic competitiveness. The immense processing power of quantum computers also raises ethical and privacy concerns, as they could be used to analyse large datasets, potentially infringing on individual privacy rights through mass data collection and analysis. Moreover, the environmental impact of quantum computers, particularly as the technology scales, could be significant. Ensuring the sustainable development and operation of quantum computing infrastructure will be crucial to mitigating these environmental concerns. The path to a quantum- resistant future is filled with challenges, but proactive measures and collaboration across the industry can pave the way for secure and sustainable technological advancements.

Impact of changing privacy laws globally

The advent of advanced technologies, including quantum computing, has significant implications for the global landscape of privacy laws and regulations, especially for startups. These emerging technologies pose new challenges for Chief Technology Officers (CTOs), who must navigate an increasingly complex regulatory environment. The impact on privacy laws and the strategies that CTOs can employ to address these challenges can be expanded upon as follows:

1) Evolving Privacy Regulations and Startup Challenges:

In the current global context, privacy laws like the European Union's General Data Protection Regulation (GDPR) and the California Consumer Privacy Act (CCPA) in the United States set stringent standards for data protection and privacy. For startups, complying with these diverse and often complex regulations can be particularly challenging, especially when operating across multiple jurisdictions. The cost of compliance is high, and the penalties for non-compliance can be severe, including substantial fines and significant reputational damage. Adding to these complexities, the advent of quantum computing poses a new challenge as it has the potential to undermine existing data protection measures, rendering traditional encryption and security protocols obsolete. This evolving landscape necessitates that startups not only keep abreast of regulatory requirements but also stay ahead of technological advancements to safeguard their data effectively.

2) The Role of CTOs in Navigating Privacy Laws:

Chief Technology Officers (CTOs) play a vital role in ensuring that startups comply with current privacy laws and stay ahead of potential changes brought about by advancements in technology, such as quantum computing. This responsibility involves staying informed about technological trends, understanding how they might impact data privacy, and anticipating changes in legislation. CTOs need to ensure that their company's data handling and processing practices are transparent and comply with existing regulations. To future-proof the startup against evolving threats, it is crucial for CTOs to proactively invest in research and development of quantum-resistant encryption methods and data security practices. By doing so, they not only safeguard the company's data but also build trust with customers and stakeholders, positioning the startup as a leader in data privacy and security.

3) Building a Privacy-Centric Culture in Startups:

CTOs should advocate for a privacy-centric culture within the organisation by implementing regular training and awareness programs for employees, emphasising the importance of data privacy and the implications of regulatory non-compliance. Developing internal policies and practices that prioritise data privacy is crucial for mitigating risks. This includes applying privacy-by-design principles in product development and ensuring that privacy considerations are integrated at every stage. Additionally, collaboration with legal and compliance teams is essential to understand the nuances of privacy laws and to ensure that technological solutions align with legal requirements. This comprehensive approach ensures that data privacy is a fundamental aspect of the company's operations, fostering trust and security for both the organisation and its stakeholders.

4) Strategic Partnerships and Compliance Tools:

For startups, forming strategic partnerships with legal experts and cybersecurity firms is crucial, as it provides valuable insights and support in navigating the complex landscape of privacy laws. These partnerships can help startups understand and comply with various regulations, avoiding potential legal issues and building a strong foundation for growth. Additionally, utilising compliance tools and software can automate parts of the compliance process, such as data mapping, privacy impact assessments, and consent management. This automation significantly reduces the administrative burden on startups, allowing them to focus more on their core business activities. Engaging in industry forums and regulatory discussions is another important step for startups. By participating in these forums, startups can have a voice in shaping future privacy regulations and standards, especially in areas impacted by emerging technologies like quantum computing. This proactive approach not only helps startups stay ahead of regulatory changes but also positions them as thought leaders in their industry. Overall, these strategies collectively enhance a startup's ability to manage privacy and compliance effectively, fostering trust and credibility with customers and stakeholders.

In conclusion, the impact of quantum computing and other emerging technologies on privacy laws presents both a challenge and an opportunity for startups. By taking a proactive, informed, and strategic approach, CTOs can guide their organisations through this evolving landscape, ensuring compliance and securing a competitive edge in the market.

Internet of Things (IoT)

The expanding landscape of the Internet of Things (IoT) brings with it a multitude of security risks. As more devices become interconnected, the potential for vulnerabilities and attacks increases significantly. Below are critical risks associated with IoT security, outlined in a point-wise format:

1. **Increased Attack Surface:** The sheer number of IoT devices, expected to reach billions, vastly expands the attack surface for cyber threats. Each connected device, from smart thermostats to industrial sensors, can potentially serve as an entry point for cyberattacks.
2. **Insecure Device Design and Manufacturing:** Many IoT devices lack robust security features, often due to cost constraints or a lack of security expertise among manufacturers. Devices may be released with insecure default settings, unencrypted data transmissions, and without the capability for security updates.
3. **Lack of Regular Updates and Patch Management:** IoT devices often have longer life cycles than typical computing devices, but may not receive regular software updates or patches. This leaves them vulnerable to known exploits long after they have been identified.
4. **Data Privacy Concerns:** IoT devices can collect vast amounts of personal data, raising concerns about privacy and data protection. Without proper safeguards, this data can be accessed or intercepted by unauthorised parties.
5. **Insufficient Authentication and Authorisation Controls:** Weak authentication processes, like simple passwords, are standard in IoT devices. Lack of robust access controls can allow attackers to gain control over devices quickly.
6. **Network Security Vulnerabilities:** IoT devices are often integrated into existing networks, but may not align with existing network

security protocols. Compromised devices can be used to launch attacks on other parts of the network or serve as a gateway for attackers.

7. **Risks Associated with Device Interoperability:** The ability of IoT devices to interact with various other devices and systems can introduce new vulnerabilities. Malfunctioning or compromised devices could disrupt the operation of other interconnected systems.

8. **Supply Chain Vulnerabilities:** The global and complex supply chains involved in IoT device production can introduce security vulnerabilities at various stages. Attackers may target any point in the supply chain to compromise the security of the device.

9. **Lack of Standardisation in IoT Security:** There is currently a lack of universally accepted standards and regulations specifically for IoT security. This results in inconsistent security practices and makes it difficult to ensure a baseline level of security across devices.

10. **Resource Constraints in IoT Devices:** Many IoT devices have limited processing power and memory, which restricts the use of advanced security measures. This limitation makes it challenging to implement strong encryption or run sophisticated security software.

11. **Physical Security Threats:** The physical accessibility of many IoT devices makes them vulnerable to tampering and physical attacks. Compromised physical security can lead to unauthorised access to data or network systems.

Addressing these risks requires a multifaceted approach involving secure design practices, regular updates, robust authentication and authorisation measures, and the development of industry-wide security standards. As the IoT landscape continues to grow, the need for comprehensive security solutions becomes increasingly critical to protect against evolving threats.

Unmanned Aerial Vehicles (UAVs)

Drones, also known as Unmanned Aerial Vehicles (UAVs), have become increasingly prevalent in both commercial and recreational applications. However, their rising use brings with it a range of security risks that need to be addressed. Here are some key security risks associated with drones, expanded in a point-wise format:

1. **Unauthorised Surveillance and Espionage:** Drones equipped with cameras and other sensors can be used for unauthorised surveillance, infringing on privacy and potentially gathering sensitive information. They pose a risk of corporate espionage, as they can quickly fly over private property to capture confidential business data.

2. **Vulnerability to Hacking and Cyber Attacks:** Drones, being wireless devices, are susceptible to hacking. This includes intercepting and altering the communication link between the drone and its controller. Hackers can gain control of a drone, alter its flight path, or even use it to conduct malicious activities.

3. **Risk of Physical Harm:** Drones can inadvertently or intentionally collide with objects or people, leading to injuries or damage. The risk of physical harm increases in densely populated areas or near critical infrastructures like airports.

4. **Use in Terrorist Activities:** Drones can be used for terrorist attacks by carrying and deploying explosives or other harmful substances. Their ability to reach secure and crowded locations makes them a potential tool for such malicious activities.

5. **Data Theft and Leaks:** Drones can be used to steal data from unsecured wireless networks. They can hover near a building and intercept unencrypted Wi-Fi signals. Drones themselves, if not properly secured, can be a source of data leaks, especially those that store flight data and multimedia content.

6. **Interference with Air Traffic**: Unauthorised drone operations near airports can interfere with air traffic, posing a significant risk to public safety. Incidents of drones flying in restricted airspaces have already led to disruptions in commercial flights.

7. **Legal and Regulatory Non-Compliance:** The use of drones is subject to varying regulations across different jurisdictions, which may include restrictions on flight zones, data collection, and privacy. Non-compliance with these regulations can lead to legal issues and penalties for individuals and companies using drones.

8. **Disruption of Sensitive Ecosystems**: Drones can inadvertently disrupt wildlife and sensitive ecosystems, mainly when used in protected natural areas. Their presence and noise can stress wildlife, leading to changes in natural behaviours and habitats.

9. **Manipulation of Media and Information:** Footage or data collected by drones can be manipulated to spread misinformation or propaganda. This poses a risk in terms of influencing public opinion or spreading false information.

10. **Dependency and Reliability Issues:** Over-reliance on drones for critical tasks can lead to vulnerabilities if the drone technology fails or is compromised. Ensuring redundancies and having backup systems in place is necessary to mitigate this risk.

To mitigate these risks, it is crucial to implement robust security measures, including encrypted communication channels, secure data storage, and adherence to legal and regulatory standards. Additionally, raising awareness about responsible drone usage and establishing clear operational guidelines are essential steps in ensuring the safe integration of drones into various sectors.

Future Cybersecurity Risks

The landscape of cybersecurity is continuously evolving, and organisations face a myriad of potential risks in the future. Here is a list of future cybersecurity risks that organisations should be aware of:

1) **Advanced Persistent Threats (APTs):**

   - Sophisticated, prolonged cyber-attacks aimed at specific entities to steal data or disrupt operations, often backed by nation-states or large criminal organisations. APTs represent a significant threat to organisations due to their highly targeted and sustained nature. Well-funded and sophisticated adversaries, such as nation-states or large criminal syndicates, typically conduct these attacks. They are characterised by their stealth and persistence, aiming to gain prolonged access to a network without being detected.

   - The goal of APTs can vary from espionage (stealing sensitive or classified information) to sabotage (disrupting critical operations).

They often involve a complex blend of tactics, including social engineering, zero-day exploits, and advanced malware.

- Organisations may find it challenging to detect APTs because they often use legitimate credentials and mimic normal network activities. This type of threat requires a robust defence strategy, including advanced threat detection systems, continuous monitoring, and regular security audits.
- To mitigate APTs, organisations also need to focus on employee training and awareness, as human error or insider threats can often be the weak link that APT actors exploit to gain access to corporate networks.

2) AI-Powered Cyber Attacks:

- The use of artificial intelligence by attackers to automate target selection, identify vulnerabilities, and optimise breach strategies, making attacks more efficient and more challenging to detect. The use of AI and machine learning by cybercriminals is a rapidly growing concern. AI can automate tasks like scanning for system vulnerabilities, making phishing attacks more convincing, or even creating malware that adapts to avoid detection.
- AI-powered attacks can analyse vast amounts of data quickly to identify potential targets and tailor attacks to specific individuals or systems, increasing the success rate of breaches.
- Such attacks can also rapidly adapt to defensive measures, learning from each interaction to avoid future detection. This makes AI-powered attacks more resilient and more challenging to combat with traditional cybersecurity measures.
- To counter AI-powered threats, organisations need to invest in AI-based security solutions themselves, which can predict and identify patterns indicative of AI-driven attacks. However, this also creates an AI arms race between attackers and defenders, constantly pushing the boundaries of what's possible in cybersecurity.

3) Quantum Computing:

The potential ability of quantum computers to break traditional encryption methods poses significant risks to data security and confidentiality.

4) Supply Chain Attacks:

Cyber-attacks target less secure elements in the supply chain, exploiting third-party vulnerabilities to compromise larger, more secure targets.

5) IoT Device Vulnerabilities:

As the number of connected IoT devices grows, so does the attack surface, with many devices lacking adequate security measures.

6) Deepfakes and Disinformation:

The use of AI-generated deepfakes to create convincing but false information, which can be used for phishing attacks, misinformation campaigns, or to damage reputations.

7) Cloud Vulnerabilities:

As more data and operations move to the cloud, vulnerabilities in cloud infrastructure or misconfigured cloud services can lead to significant data breaches.

8) Mobile Device Exploits:

With the increasing reliance on mobile devices in the corporate environment, they have become attractive targets for cyber-attacks, including app-based vulnerabilities and mobile phishing attacks.

9) Ransomware Evolution:

The continuous evolution of ransomware tactics, including double extortion schemes where attackers both encrypt data and threaten to release it publicly.

10) Insider Threats:

Risks posed by current or former employees, contractors, or business partners, either maliciously or inadvertently, can lead to significant security breaches.

11) 5G Network Vulnerabilities:

The rollout of 5G networks, while offering improved speed and connectivity, also opens new avenues for cyberattacks due to increased connectivity and potential vulnerabilities.

12) Increased Regulation and Compliance Challenges:

As cybersecurity regulations become more stringent, organisations will face challenges in maintaining compliance, with potential legal and financial ramifications for non-compliance.

13) Social Engineering and Phishing Attacks:

The sophistication of social engineering and phishing attacks is likely to increase, exploiting human psychology to gain unauthorised access to sensitive information.

14) Smart City and Critical Infrastructure Attacks:

Cyber-attacks targeting critical infrastructure and smart city technologies can have widespread implications for public safety and services.

15) Machine Learning and Data Poisoning:

Attacks targeting machine learning systems through data poisoning or model manipulation, potentially leading to flawed decision-making or system behaviours.

16) Cross-Platform and Cross-Device Attacks:

The interconnected nature of devices and platforms can allow cyber threats to move laterally across different systems, exploiting vulnerabilities in one to compromise another.

17) Erosion of Trust in Digital Systems:

As cyber-attacks become more prevalent and sophisticated, there is a risk of eroding public trust in digital systems and technologies.

Organisations must remain vigilant and proactive in their cybersecurity strategies, continually adapting to these evolving risks to protect their data, assets, and reputation.

The integration of Artificial Intelligence (AI) into cyber attacks marks a significant escalation in the cyber threat landscape. Attackers leveraging

AI tools can automate and optimise various stages of their attacks, making them more efficient, effective, and challenging to detect. AI algorithms can be used to scan for vulnerabilities across large networks, identify high-value targets, and even customise phishing campaigns with unprecedented precision.

This automation allows cybercriminals to launch large-scale attacks with minimal effort, potentially overwhelming traditional cybersecurity defences. AI can analyse patterns in security systems, learn from each interaction, and adapt to avoid detection, making it a formidable tool in the hands of sophisticated attackers.

One of the most concerning aspects of AI-powered cyber-attacks is their ability to evolve. Unlike static, rule-based attack methods, AI-driven attacks can continuously learn and adjust their strategies based on feedback from their environment. For instance, an AI-driven malware could alter its behaviour to evade detection by antivirus software, or an AI-based phishing tool could refine its techniques based on the responses of its targets.

This capacity for rapid adaptation means that AI-powered attacks can persist longer and have a higher success rate than traditional attacks. Furthermore, AI can be used to sift through vast amounts of stolen data quickly, extracting valuable information more efficiently than ever before.

In response to this growing threat, organisations must adopt a more dynamic approach to cybersecurity. This involves not only deploying AI-based security solutions themselves, which can predict, identify, and respond to AI-driven attacks, but also fostering a culture of continuous learning and adaptation among their cybersecurity teams. Cybersecurity professionals need to stay abreast of the latest developments in AI and machine learning to counteract AI-driven threats effectively. Additionally, organisations should consider collaborating with others in their industry and participating in information-sharing networks to gain insights into emerging threats and best practices. As the use of AI in cyber-attacks becomes more prevalent, the only viable defence will be a proactive, intelligent approach that evolves in lockstep with the threats.

Furthermore, AI-driven attacks can process and analyse vast amounts of data at an unprecedented pace, making them particularly effective in identifying vulnerabilities and extracting valuable information from large datasets. For instance, AI can be used in sophisticated phishing operations, where it tailors deceptive messages based on the target's behaviour and preferences, significantly increasing the likelihood of success. Additionally, AI can enhance the capabilities of malware, allowing it to navigate a network intelligently, identify the most critical systems, and decide the optimal time to launch an attack or exfiltrate data.

To effectively defend against these advanced threats, organisations need to adopt equally sophisticated cybersecurity strategies. This involves not only implementing AI-based defence mechanisms but also fostering a culture of continuous learning and vigilance within their cybersecurity teams. Cybersecurity professionals must stay informed about the latest developments in AI and machine learning to build defences that can anticipate and counter AI-driven attacks. Regular training and updating of security protocols are crucial in keeping pace with the rapidly evolving threat landscape.

Moreover, collaboration and information sharing between organisations and across industries play a vital role in building a collective defence against AI-powered attacks. Sharing insights about emerging threats, attack patterns, and effective defence strategies can help build a more robust and resilient cybersecurity ecosystem. As AI becomes an increasingly common tool in the arsenal of cyber attackers, a proactive and adaptive approach to cybersecurity, grounded in advanced technology and industry collaboration, is essential to protect sensitive data and maintain the integrity of digital infrastructures.

Deepfake Technology

The emergence of deepfake technology, which leverages advanced AI algorithms to create hyper-realistic but entirely fabricated audio and visual content, represents a new frontier in the spread of disinformation and digital deception. This technology's ability to convincingly mimic individuals in videos or audio recordings makes it a potent tool for creating misleading or fraudulent content. As the technology becomes more accessible and sophisticated, the potential for its misuse increases significantly. Deepfakes can be employed in a variety of malicious ways, including impersonating public figures or corporate leaders to spread false information, manipulating stock markets by fabricating announcements or news or damaging the reputations of individuals and organisations through the creation of fake compromising content. The credibility and trust in digital content are thereby severely undermined, posing a significant challenge to individuals, corporations, and even democratic institutions.

The increasing difficulty in distinguishing deepfakes from authentic content adds a complex layer to the challenge of managing this threat. Traditional methods of verifying the authenticity of audio and video content are becoming less effective as deepfake technology evolves. This presents a critical issue for organisations, as decision-making often relies on the integrity of such media. To combat this, organisations must not only invest in emerging detection technologies that can identify subtle inconsistencies or anomalies in deepfakes but also foster a heightened sense of awareness and scepticism among employees and stakeholders. Educating staff about the nature of deepfakes, the techniques used to create them, and their potential impact is crucial. This education can empower individuals to critically assess the authenticity of the media they consume, particularly in a professional context where the stakes are high.

In response to the deepfake challenge, organisations must implement robust verification processes, especially in situations where significant decisions are based on digital media. This could involve multiple methods of verification for audio and video communications, such as cross-referencing with other sources, confirming the identity of individuals through separate communication channels, or using blockchain technology to verify the origin and integrity of digital content. Establishing robust internal protocols and guidelines for media verification can help mitigate the risks associated with deepfakes. Additionally, organisations should consider engaging with external experts and investing in specialised software capable of detecting deepfakes. As the technology continues to evolve, staying ahead in detection and verification methods will be vital in protecting against the misuse of deepfake technology and maintaining the integrity of digital communication.

18) Cross-Device Attacks

The emergence of cross-platform and cross-device attacks represents a significant evolution in the cybersecurity threat landscape. These attacks transcend the boundaries of individual devices or platforms, exploiting the interconnected nature of modern digital environments. In a cross-platform attack, cybercriminals exploit vulnerabilities that exist across different operating systems or software platforms.

This approach allows them to target a broader range of victims with a single type of exploit. For instance, a vulnerability in a widely used software library could be exploited to attack systems running on Windows, macOS, and Linux simultaneously. These attacks are particularly challenging to defend against because they leverage commonalities in code or functionality that are present across multiple platforms.

Cross-device attacks take advantage of the growing interconnectedness of various types of devices within networks. As the Internet of Things (IoT) expands and more devices become 'smart' and connected, the potential for these attacks increases. In a cross-device scenario, an attacker might compromise a seemingly innocuous device, like a smart thermostat or a connected printer, and use it as a foothold to infiltrate more secure parts of the network.

This type of attack is insidious because it uses less secure devices as gateways to more valuable targets, like corporate servers or sensitive data repositories. The diversity of devices and the variability in their security postures make it challenging to ensure consistent protection across the entire network.

The complexity of defending against cross-platform and cross-device attacks is compounded by the diversity of software and hardware involved. Traditional security measures are often designed with a specific platform or device type in mind, making them less effective against attacks that bridge these divides. This challenge is exacerbated in environments where there is a mix of legacy and modern systems, each with its own set of vulnerabilities and security requirements. Organisations need to adopt a holistic security approach that considers the entire ecosystem of devices and platforms.

This approach should include regular vulnerability assessments and updates, network segmentation to limit the spread of attacks, and the use of advanced threat detection and response systems capable of identifying and mitigating threats that move laterally across different systems.

To effectively counter cross-platform and cross-device attacks, organisations must also foster a culture of security awareness among their employees and users. This involves educating them about the risks associated with different types of devices and platforms and the best practices for securing them. Additionally, there is a need for greater collaboration between device manufacturers, software developers, and security professionals to address these threats.

By sharing information about vulnerabilities and attack methodologies and by working together to develop more robust security standards, stakeholders across the digital ecosystem can enhance their collective defence against these increasingly sophisticated and far-reaching cyber threats. In an era where the lines between different platforms and devices are increasingly blurred, a unified and collaborative approach to cybersecurity is essential to protect against the multifaceted threats posed by cross-platform and cross-device attacks.

Usage of Mobile Devices and Evolving Threats

The growing reliance on mobile devices in corporate environments has made them increasingly attractive targets for cybercriminals. The ubiquitous use of smartphones, tablets, and other mobile devices in professional settings presents a unique set of challenges and vulnerabilities. One of the primary risks is exposure to app-based vulnerabilities. Many business operations rely on various applications, which can include everything from communication tools to financial transaction platforms. However, these apps can contain security flaws, either in their design or due to the way they interact with the device's operating system. Attackers can exploit these vulnerabilities to gain unauthorised access to confidential corporate information, execute malicious code, or even take control of the device itself.

Phishing Attacks

Another significant threat comes from mobile phishing attacks. Unlike traditional phishing attacks that typically occur via email, mobile phishing can occur through text messages (SMS), social media apps, or even through fake apps and malicious websites accessed via the mobile browser. The smaller screen size and simplified user interface of mobile devices can make it more difficult for users to recognise suspicious content.

Furthermore, mobile users often operate in a context of more excellent distraction and urgency, which can lead to hurried and less cautious decision-making. This environment makes mobile devices particularly susceptible to phishing attacks, which can result in the compromise of personal and corporate data.

How To Mitigate These Risks?

To mitigate these risks, organisations must implement comprehensive mobile device management (MDM) policies and solutions. MDM allows IT administrators to manage and secure mobile devices that access corporate data remotely. This includes enforcing strong password policies, configuring devices to lock automatically, and remotely wiping data on lost or stolen devices.

Additionally, organisations can use application management tools to control which apps can be installed on corporate devices, ensuring that only verified and secure apps are used for business purposes. Regular updates and patches for both apps and the mobile operating system are crucial in protecting against known vulnerabilities.

Alongside technical measures, educating employees about mobile security risks is equally important. This includes training on how to recognise phishing attempts, the importance of using secure Wi-Fi networks, and the risks associated with downloading apps from unofficial sources. Employees should be encouraged to report any suspicious activity on their mobile devices immediately. Furthermore, organisations should consider the adoption of a 'zero-trust' security model, where every access request is fully authenticated, authorised, and encrypted before access is granted, regardless of the user's location or device. By combining robust technology solutions with informed and vigilant user behaviour, organisations can significantly reduce the risk posed by mobile device exploits in the corporate environment.

The increasing prevalence and sophistication of cyber-attacks pose a significant threat not just to the security of digital systems but also to the public's trust in these technologies. As individuals and organisations increasingly rely on digital platforms for essential services like banking, healthcare, communication, and commerce, the impact of cyber breaches becomes more profound.

High-profile incidents involving data breaches, identity theft, and financial fraud have already shaken consumer confidence. The fear that personal data may not be secure can lead individuals to be hesitant in adopting new technologies or fully engaging with online services. This erosion of trust can have far-reaching consequences, slowing the progress of digital innovation and impacting the growth of digital economies. In a world where digital interactions are becoming the norm, the assurance of security and privacy is paramount to maintaining public confidence in these systems.

The ripple effects of this erosion of trust extend beyond individual consumers to impact businesses and governments. For businesses, a breach in security can lead to a loss of customer trust, which is often more challenging to recover than the financial losses incurred. In the digital age, a company's reputation is closely tied to its ability to protect customer data. A single breach can lead to long-term brand damage and a loss of competitive edge. For governments, maintaining the trust of citizens is crucial for the effective implementation of digital initiatives, such as e-governance services, digital IDs, and innovative city projects. When public trust in digital systems is compromised, it can lead to resistance against digitalisation efforts, hindering the advancement and potential benefits of these initiatives.

To counteract this erosion of trust, a multifaceted approach is required. This includes implementing robust cybersecurity measures, ensuring transparency in how data is collected, used, and protected, and responding quickly and effectively to any breaches that do occur. Regular audits and compliance with international data protection standards can help reassure the public about the safety of their data.

Education and awareness campaigns are also critical in helping the public understand the measures being taken to protect their digital information and their role in maintaining personal data security. Furthermore, collaboration between the public and private sectors can play a pivotal role in enhancing the overall security of digital ecosystems. By taking these steps, it's possible to rebuild and maintain the trust that is essential for the continued growth and sustainability of digital systems and technologies.

As we conclude our exploration of the future of cybersecurity, we recognise that the field is evolving at an unprecedented pace, driven by rapid technological advancements and an ever-changing threat landscape. The emergence of trends like quantum computing, IoT security, AI-powered cyber-attacks, and the increasing sophistication of digital threats signals a pivotal shift in the way we approach cybersecurity.

These advancements are not merely technological phenomena; they represent a fundamental transformation in the fabric of digital security. Quantum computing, for instance, challenges the very foundations of current cryptographic practices. At the same time, the proliferation of IoT devices expands the cybersecurity battleground to include an array of new, often less secure devices. In this context, the role of cybersecurity becomes more critical than ever, underpinning the safety and integrity of our digital world.

For startups and established organisations alike, these trends necessitate a reevaluation of cybersecurity strategies. The traditional perimeter-based approach to security is no longer sufficient in a landscape where threats can emerge from any connected device anywhere in the world. The future of cybersecurity lies in adopting a more holistic, proactive approach that integrates advanced technologies, continuous monitoring, and a culture of security awareness throughout the organisation.

As AI becomes a tool in the arsenal of both defenders and attackers, the race to outsmart the adversary will intensify. Organisations will need to leverage AI not only to predict and prevent attacks but also to respond to them swiftly and effectively when they occur.

The potential of quantum computing to break current encryption methods also raises urgent questions about the future of data privacy and security. The transition to quantum-resistant cryptographic methods is not merely a technical challenge; it is a strategic imperative that requires significant investment and collaboration across industries and governments.

Similarly, the growing reliance on IoT devices calls for a reimagined approach to device security, one that emphasises secure design, regular updates, and robust network protections. In navigating these changes, startups will find that agility and adaptability are their greatest assets, allowing them to respond quickly to emerging threats and incorporate new security measures.

Conclusion

In summary, the future of cybersecurity is a landscape of both challenges and opportunities. As emerging technologies redefine the parameters of digital threats, they also offer new tools and approaches for defence. The organisations that will thrive in this new era are those that recognise the importance of cybersecurity not as an afterthought but as a fundamental component of their operations and strategy. By staying informed, adaptable, and proactive, startups can navigate this evolving landscape, turning potential vulnerabilities into strengths and ensuring their resilience in the face of an increasingly complex array of cyber threats.

As we reach the end of "Securing Your Startup," it's clear that navigating the digital landscape requires more than just innovative ideas and determination. It demands a robust security framework, proactive measures, and a deep understanding of the evolving threat landscape. Throughout this book, we've explored the essential components of cybersecurity, from building a secure infrastructure and integrating security into your DevOps practices to understanding the importance of data protection and regulatory compliance.

We've delved into the intricacies of securing cloud environments, the critical role of encryption, and the necessity of continuous monitoring and incident response. Real-world case studies have highlighted how prioritising security can be a significant market differentiator, showcasing startups that have successfully leveraged robust security measures to build trust and gain a competitive edge.

The journey of securing a startup is akin to embarking on an adventurous expedition. It involves careful planning, the right tools, constant vigilance, and the ability to adapt to new challenges. By integrating security into the very DNA of your startup, you not only protect your assets but also foster a culture of trust and resilience.

Remember, the digital world is constantly evolving, and so should your security strategies. Stay informed, stay prepared, and continue to prioritise security at every step of your startup's growth. With the insights and strategies outlined in this book, you are well-equipped to face the challenges and seize the opportunities that lie ahead. Here's to building a secure and successful startup that stands the test of time!

Testimonial –

"Securing Startups" is an outstanding book authored by my friend Sanil Nadkarni. It's not just theory—it's a practical playbook. Any DevOps engineer or security enthusiast can pick it up and immediately start applying what Sanil has mastered through securing multiple startups. A must-read for those serious about building secure foundations from day one.

— Amit Ghodekar - Global CISO Aramex.

Testimonial from Hilal Done – Ex-CISO Razor Pay

I am writing to wholeheartedly endorse the upcoming book authored by a remarkable Chief Information Security Officer (CISO) and a close friend of mine, whose expertise in managing security in startup environments is unparalleled.

In a landscape where startups are increasingly targeted by sophisticated cyber threats, his book emerges as a beacon of practical wisdom and strategic guidance. His battle-hardened experiences, drawn from managing security across various scales in startups, offer invaluable insights that are as rare as they are crucial.

What sets him apart is not just his technical prowess but also his ability to translate complex security concepts into actionable strategies that are accessible to startup teams of all sizes and technical backgrounds. His leadership skills, combined with a deep understanding of both the challenges and opportunities unique to startups, make his perspectives especially relevant and compelling.

For any startup looking to fortify its defences and navigate the intricate world of cybersecurity, this book is an indispensable resource. It reflects the author's talent for balancing robust security practices with the agility and innovation that startups require.

In summary, this book is a testament to his exceptional skills and dedication to the field of information security. It's an essential read for anyone involved in or aspiring to be part of the startup.